BRIDGETT MADDOX

DIVINE PURPOSE WITH MANIFESTED POWER
YOUR DATE WITH DESTINY

outskirts
press

Table of Contents

Foreword
Divine Purpose with
Manifested Power

WE ARE SENT here to live life fully, to live abundantly, to find
joy in our own creation, to experience both failures and suc-
cesses, to use free will to expand and magnify our lives. Like a
butterfly this end time Prophet has went through a near death
experience while in fact, this dying experience has propelled
her to walk in the supernatural power that is desperately needed to reeducate ourselves for a life of winning. We are spiritual
beings, as well as, biological machines. Many of our society
problems, include health care crisis, death with dignity and the
cult of greed, which has bankrupted our economy. The nation-
al shame of homeless women and children. Many lack understanding that we are SPIRITUAL BEINGS who are mutually

dependent upon each other. This woman of God has allowed God to shape her into the image of Jesus Christ, for such a time as this. God has anointed her with Power and Authority.

Dr.W.F.Hughes
Pastor of Power and Authority Tabernacle D.M.

THE DIVINE (PERFECT) WILL OF GOD

PLACE OF DESTINY will create a greatness that will be birthed inside of you. In Ruth 2:5, Ruth is in her set divine purpose for her life. Notice she is found doing the will of the Father. She is not worried about her current state. She is being obedient to the voice of God. After she obeys the spirit by way of Naomi giving her instruction to go and work the field, her promise meets her. Her perfect will would not have come to pass had she stayed in her unharvested place. Boaz was the perfect will of God for her life. Be willing to become too stretched in order for this to happen; there has to be a tearing down and pulling away of the things that the flesh craves. Galatians 5:24 tells us to crucify our flesh after we have committed our lives to serving the Lord; does this sinful nature of our old man die? Note this is a constant daily part of the flesh. We must purposely die to our sinful nature. This comes by renewing our minds aligned in scripture. Be willing to go in that place of uncharted territory. Resist your fears and God will grace you. Don't compromise God's best for a quick fix. Wait on the Lord! Part of being in the divine will is patience. *Patience* is defined as a person's ability to wait something out or endure something tedious without getting riled up. "Patience is not simply the ability to wait; it's how we behave while we are waiting" (Joyce Meyer). This is a powerful look at how the children of Israel murmured and complained. One could concur that their patience was not being executed in faith. We know the result: God kept them there many years. Step out, and in your place of provision God will meet you at your point of need. God promises us blessings for living righteously. Deuteronomy 28:1–3 points out that we will be in a great position for living right. Obedience will determine our altitude. Christians should walk in Love at all times. Be quick to repent. Unforgiveness will stop God's best from flowing into your life. Obedience is another key. What is obedience? Obedience is obeying God's laws and commands. Step out and your place of provision will meet you at your point of need. Oftentimes we will walk according to our flesh and we will reap the things of the flesh. But place yourself in the things of the spirit to produce a harvest of fulfillment. Living life with a desired expectancy that greatness will prevail over any hardship that the enemy tries to use. I remember when I had owned four salons, and on the fourth one I thought: God, you brought me back around to my original place of destination. That was my very first hair salon, and the owner of the shopping center's wife was a client whose hair I had serviced for years, and her husband would always request that I come back. But you see, God will never take us backwards. I did not seek God's approval of this relocation. My flesh wanted a quick fix, cheap rent. No stress. So it seemed; little did I know what was on the other side. So it seemed it was economic hardships. You see that was a setup from the enemy. Satan knows there is destiny inside of each and every one of you. To no avail; what was once a blessing in 1989 had now become a curse because the fruit that was once there had dried up. The brook had dried up. It was in my obedience after toiling with God—should I leave, should I stay?—I said no. Enough is enough, I had a mandate to leave in 2006. God said my life depended on it. If you have a word like that, you will certainly run. I was like the widow woman: God met me at my place of provision. There was work for me to do in the Humble area, and the Holy Spirit had instructed me to go into that uncharted territory. I had to sell all that I had; by instruction of a prophet God had instructed me to move months ago. Not only did I have enough resources to move, but I was able to cancel some debts that were behind. That's the power of God. My obedience produced a harvested field of fruit. My business doubled in revenue the year after the move, after leaving the land of Egypt. Canaan was the prophetic place of destiny. What is your prophetic place? Could it be your current dwelling? Or is God challenging you to elevate yourself and step into the unknown? Now you're talking Faith. It doesn't require a level of faith to stay in familiar territory. Be willing to move with the cloud. Don't stay with the cloud in a dry place if the cloud has set out to another location. There are people who will try to detour you off your road of promise. Always line it up with the word of the Lord. If God doesn't tell you, then wait on peace from the throne. Never move until you have peace in your spirit to proceed. One should not move forward with a desired assignment. God is not obligated to bless you if you go on your own accord. Be led by the spirit at all times! Don't go with those that don't have the heart of the Father. Prayer: Dear God, help me to discern Good versus Evil; grant me wisdom, knowledge, and understanding to rightly divide the truth of your word, and apply those biblical promises so I may walk victoriously. In Jesus' name, Amen. Opposition will arise when you go into the place called "The Blessed Place of Destination." Remember, Satan will try his best to knock you off course, but you must be planted like a tree. Psalms 1:3. Though the storms of life and circumstances will come, you must Never Quit. Prayer: Lord Jesus, help me to bridge my place of "Now" to walk into my place of "There"; rest me, Holy Spirit, under your precious wings. Thank you, Father, for loving me in the place of destiny. I embrace my next place of destiny In Jesus' Name.... I expect provision to follow me as I take this Journey. Comfort me in this place of my new level; I know trials are evident but with you I can win...Hallelujah. Allow the Holy Spirit to guide you. Daily dispatch the angels to go before you to create the way of your paths. This will reduce the level of hindrances in the earth realm. Oftentimes as believers, we don't realize the power that we have with our tongue. You could actually curse yourself with foolish talking. For example: "I'm not gonna ever make it." "I'm catching a cold." "If it's not one thing it's another." How many times have we used foolish talking? Maybe we did not know we had not been taught in our arenas of life—culture's religious places. It's time that we begin to ponder on what it is we are thinking about before we speak. Decree life. Speak the word! Over yourself, over your problems, finances, health, and over your innermost being which is your Spirit. It's well. In Jesus' name. I am healed in Jesus' name. I will come out of debt. I am the head and not the tail. I will lend to Nations but borrow from none. Speak your desired end result, but remember to search the scriptures and pray the word over your situation. It will produce results every time. "My children are mighty in the land" Psalms 112. Begin to meditate on the scriptures and see what God is speaking to you. Seek the master's face for divine revelation to create a natural manifestation in the earth realm. We have been given our Spiritual Access to gain entry to the kingdom via "The Word of God." No matter what comes at you, you must be committed to praying, fasting, and seeking God for your life. Satan will do his best to get you to throw your hand in, but you must not stop. You have to stand strong against the wiles of the Devil and know that with God on your side, you will win this Faith Fight. Power is available; the greater one is working on the inside of you. In this we will win. Adversity will come, trials will come, testing will come. PRESS, PURSUE, and DREAM into your destiny. Only God can make you believe that we are able to take the land of giants, and possess they had great faith; we must be able to take the land reference that Joshua and Caleb will go into the land of giants and Possess they had great faith—we must begin to see through our eyes of faith. Take dominion, territory, and possess all that God has promised us. What would have happened if Joshua and Caleb had turned back before they scouted out the land? What was the element that they both possessed? It was the "Power of Agreement." Which brings me to my next point. Watch out for those people of no belief. They are negative and realistically they will block you from being all that you could possibly be. Ask God to help you to examine your relationships you have formed. If those friends or relatives are critical and toxic relationships, then you must remove yourself from these people. It does not mean that you don't love them. The truth is you cannot allow the enemy to paralyze your God-given potential that could hinder where you are going. Take inventory periodically and clean your life of unhealthy relationships. Secondly, you should not be the smartest one in your circle of influence. You should always be stretched. Find a mentor. Someone who can help you to grow and go higher in the things of the spirit. Which means sometimes that person will not always tell you what you want to hear. A good mentor will always correct, rebuke, or bring reproach, but isn't that the very thing that a parent would often do to their children, because they love them and want to see them shine?... God is faithful; he will bring the right people that will be an asset into your life. You will soar to new horizons with this one principle. Unbelief must be cast down, vain imaginations that exalt against the knowledge of God. Why were the other men not persuaded that they would go in? Perhaps because of who they had walking with them. One must have people of like faith to possess. Grasshopper mentality must be completely eradicated, destroyed, annihilated completely to take control and put the enemy under our feet. It's for us to obtain our God-given potential that the enemy has stolen from us. He (the devil) will put it back sevenfold, says God; believe by faith and receive it. The violent take it by force. Silence your fears with the word. It is not an option to experience how it looks in the natural. Look through your spiritual eyes of faith. God has not given us a spirit of fear, but of love, peace, and a sound mind. Surround yourself around those people that will help you to be accountable; this will be key in reaching the highest mark that is set before you. Peace is available; the anointing will destroy the yokes of bondage in your life. Prayer: Father, reveal to us everything that we must do to release this power to work from the Spirit to produce an abundant harvest in the natural realm. In Jesus' Name, Amen. "The Faith to Faith It In." You say, "Pastor B, what is it?" Whatever you need or want. Maybe it's a desire to go to school. Age issues. Reference to Abraham when God promises him a seed. Genesis 18:13 Take God at his word and move into The Realm of Faith. What *is* faith? Faith, simply put, is It's Impossible to please God. Apply Truth by meditating on the word of God. Faith comes by hearing. Feed your faith with CDs, videos, etc. This will help to develop your spirit, so when Satan attempts to tell you things contrary to the word, you can cast it down with the sword of the spirit, which is the word of the Lord! The faith to faith it in? You say, "What is that?" You will only go as far as your faith will allow you to go. What do you mean? For example, there was a time when my business had to operate with a great amount of money. In the natural there was no way I could have done it. But I had to faith my finances in. I believe I received according to my level of faith, because of my belief in God's word; I needed God faith to walk victoriously every day to have met that kind of budget, and guess what? God was faithful every month. This was the very issue that the woman with the issue of blood did: she believed by faith that if she could just touch the hem of Jesus garment, she could be made whole. She did press; can you imagine how weak she had to have been? She had this blood issue for twelve years; she wasn't concerned about how she felt—she knew that her blessing was in her persistence, and furthermore back in those days it was forbidden for a woman to be in public at that time of the month: she was considered unclean. She also risked being stoned to death. We know the story: she received her healing. Jesus told her, "Thou faith has made thee whole" Luke 8:43 The Bible declares that without faith it is impossible to please him (God). On the other hand, I have experienced what I call Limited Faith; I did not need faith to pay bills because I was never being stretched. You must never develop a mentality of complacency. This is enough, I don't need a larger home, this beat-up car will do. I guess my kids will never go to college. You know we have all heard these stories, or we have ourselves announced them out of the error of wrong thinking. Dream big, take the limits off, don't box yourself in. Speaking of limited faith, I remember when we were living in my husband's grandmother's home. It was a fixer-upper, but somehow I knew that a few years there to get on our feet would be great. I remember there were times when I would constantly think if I'm not careful, I could easily go into a spirit of complacency. I felt that we were not being challenged in a higher level of living. I began to seek God about a better level of living. I knew I wanted better for my children; this was a low point in our marriage. One day the Holy Spirit revealed to me that my husband had a soul tie to this home: this was the home that his grandmother raised him in, and he could not see himself beyond this life. I will never forget one night when my cousin and his wife had moved into a new house and we visited, and our son Alec Jordan stated to his dad, "No no no. Don't want to leave this house—nice nice, Daddy." I will never forget the look on Ernest's face; now at this point I had been praying for years to move out to a better location, and he was not listening to me. It was at that moment, our little baby boy uttered those words and the rest was history. Out of the mouth Babes shall speak. He immediately said to me, "Bridgett, we are moving." Glory to God. Don't worry if your prayers are not being answered; God has a way of getting them answered. Be patient and trust in the Lord. We went home and my husband began to surf the Internet, and that same day we found the home that we currently reside in. "Way to go, Alec. I have some more things I need done!" Prayer: Lord, please allow me to think only of those things that pertain to life and more abundantly In Jesus' Name. I purposely choose to allow my spirit to meditate daily on these biblical principles that have been preordained before the foundations of the earth. I WILL arise, stand strong, and walk into the Promised Land that you have set for me Isaiah 60:1. Thank you, Holy Spirit, for guiding me, and even when I fall off track, remind me with your still, small voice that I might quickly turn around and gain lost momentum. "... God from all their troubles. The Lord is the stronghold of my life of whom shall I be afraid" Psalms 13. I am confident of this. I will see the goodness of the Lord in the land of the living. Wait for the Lord, be strong and take heart and wait for the Lord. Patience produces integrity; when one is being patient, that shows true character. When a man's character is in the right perspective, this will yield integrity. Integrity is doing it God's way even if man does not agree with it. Integrity will produce streams of income and blessings. Integrity is getting to work and working a full eight hours; even if the boss is out on vacation, you will produce with tenacity as if he were present. God will honor the upright; this is his promise according to Psalms 13. Define *Integrity*: the quality of being honest and having strong moral principles, moral uprightness. I am still confident of this; I will see the goodness of the Lord in the land of the living. Wait for the Lord; be strong and take heart; be patient as the Lord begins to intervene on your behalf. Daily, speak "the Favor of God is on my life." Prosperity is available for all; God is not a respecter of persons. This is also a faith principle; you must activate this by speaking words into the atmosphere to release the blessings. Genesis 1:3 AND GOD SAID "The Rest Was History." That same power is available today, but I've heard others say, "Oh that was then." The Bible states that Jesus is the same yesterday, today, and forevermore. That will cancel out that theory. Meditate on only what the word says and omit the rest that will hinder God's best in your life. Remember: watch the power of your words!

I've told myself and my family, "Think about what you're thinking about before you speak it." Our words will be launched from here into eternity. This is for me too (smile). Jesus told Lazarus in the book to "Come forth" and it was so; he got up, gave up the dead clothes, and came out of the grave. "What is in your life that needs to be resurrected?" Romans 6:4. That same resurrecting power is available today; tap into this anointing that will be life-changing. Receive this blessing by faith. We should also know that our finances can use resurrecting. God honors obedience. The principle of the tithe will always produce the promise. According to Malachi 3:10. The tithe is holy; this will keep the Devil from devouring your seed. No one wants to work hard sowing on a field and in the end produce a field of drought and lack. This is the same principle that God has instructed every born-again believer to operate in. Watch Jehovah Jireh blow on your tenth. It's His Promise. We will reap that which we have sown. Note: Make sure that you are sowing on good ground..... That will be ministries that operate in the same spiritual principles. Sow higher into the ground so that you can go higher. I've seen too many times God protect my family's home that could have been foreclosed on. See chapter on Discerning the Voice of God. Stay in an attitude of reverence to God; he is pleased in the prosperity of his servant. Prayer: Father, I thank you that everything I do is grounded in your love. I will love, honor, and respect others, I bless those people that spitefully misuse me and I purposely choose to forgive them of their trespasses, and I pray God's blessing over them. As I forgive others, let me not forget to forgive myself for the things I should have done, or did not do. Thank you, Father, for loving us Even when we miss the Mark. In Jesus' Name, Amen.

DIVINE CONNECTIONS

DIVINE CONNECTIONS: WHAT would those possibly be? These are connections that you are connected to these connectors will bridge you into your divine purpose. These are your team players that will help you be all that God has called you to be for his kingdom. You will walk in your God-given assignment, but in order to do that , this foundational principle will help you overcome, the wrong mindset. Pharisees are in your circle of influence. Begin to ask God to reveal Divine Connections to you on this day. Start out with a new sense of awareness as to how you will get propelled into your Divine Purpose with the Power that will be already at work in you. Remember, you have the power to release this from the depth of your spirit. Ready, Set, Let's Take It.... "The violent take it by force" Matthew 11:12. "And from the days John the Baptist until now the kingdom of heaven suffereth violence, and the violence take it by force." People divinely connected to you will be an asset to you. They will bring love, peace, joy, happiness, meekness, temperance—all of these things are talked about in the book of Galatians 5:22–24 about the Fruits of the spirit. What are the fruits? Fruits are manifestations of Great things to have. This is not always tangible things; it can mean peace in your mind. A wealthy person can have influence but no JOY in their heart. Spiritually they are BROKE. The positive affirmations that your inner circle of influence will bring to you. These are your cheerleaders of your life. Also, one must be willing to receive correction and rebuke in love. A true friend or believer will tell you the good and bad even if it hurts. This correction will help you to be all that God has called you to be. Always line it up with the word…. Opinions don't count; only facts and truthfulness will be accepted. Real people won't tell you what you want to hear; there are moments when things will not always be so great, but remember God will take care of his own and he will perfect that which concerns him. He is there in the boat, in the book of Mark when the men were on the boat and the storms were raging and they grew afraid, and Jesus not knowing at the time what was happening arose to find the men in scared desperation. What did he tell the wind? Three words: "PEACE, BE STILL"…. Instantly the wind ceased. Friends, we have that same power in our mouths, yet many Christians are living defeated lives. Let's put pressure on the word.

Blessing Blockers: these are the people or Pharisees that try to hinder God's best in your life; they are jealous, envious, resentful, full of strife, and sometimes just downright evil. Stay clear of these people. They can cause major accidents on the highway to greatness. If the Holy Spirit reveals to you that they are your assignment, then Almighty God will anoint you to handle the attacks from the adversary. Negative energy tends to drain you from being all that God has called you to be. The Bible declares you will know them by the fruit they bear. Test the spirit, by the spirit, to see if they be of God. 1 John 4:2-3 Jesus has come in the flesh.... This is the Spirit with Godly attributes. "Know by faith God will lift up a standard and no Devil in Hell will come near thou Dwelling" Psalms 91. God will put the right people in your life; ask him to reveal your plan of purpose to you. Remember he is always speaking, BUT are we listening? Take the time and focus on the voice of the Master. Hidden secrets will be revealed in this state.... Remain still; he will in fact show you. I am a firm believer that nothing happens by accident; I am convinced with every fiber of my being that our paths of friendships, coworkers, employees, employers, or other meaningful connections will always have valuable relevance that will be proven in the end. I remember my Spiritual daughter TaNisha was and is still a great client of mine. She is my armor-bearer—this girl has my back. She calls me her Pastor B.... I think that is so cute. Only I would always tell her that. Anyway, one day the Holy Spirit gave me a word of knowledge that she will one day work with me in ministry. I could not in the natural even begin to fathom in my wildest dreams how this could possibly be. I was looking through my natural lenses, and it was predestined before the foundations of the world that she would help me in ministry. Note: I was not even ministering at that time. How many know if God says it, it must surely come to pass, and guess what? It did. Three years later the Lord told me to have a conference, and it would be called "**Divine Purpose with Manifested Power.**" To God Be the Glory this book was birthed out of the obedience. That's the power of God I could not begin to understand: Who, What, When, Why.... It would happen; I knew one day in His timing, not Bridgett's timing, it would happen. That was in 2005—year of grace—2007 had the conference—2009 birthed the book. What is your time line?... Create the time line that God has already given you and write the script that he has for your life.... Now its here..2017 Book released!

INTEGRITY

PSALMS 25:21 MAY integrity and Uprightness protect me, because my hope is in you. Redeem Israel O God from all their troubles. The Lord is the stronghold of my life, of whom shall I be afraid? Philippians 4:8 declares, "Whatever is true, whatever is honorable, whatever is right, whatever is pure, whatever is lovely, whatever is of good repute, if there is any excellence and if anything worthy of praise dwell on these things." I am still confident of this. I will see the goodness of the Lord in the land of the living. Wait for the Lord. Integrity will produce streams of blessings to come upon you. *Favor* is defined as God's unmerited favor in one's life. Daily speak that the favor of God is on my life. Prosperity is available for every born-again believer. God is no respecter of persons. This is also a faith principle; you must activate this by speaking the words into the atmosphere, to release the blessings. Genesis 1:3 "And God said." The rest was history. That same power is available today, but

I've heard others say, "Oh, that was then. That doesn't apply." Then why did Jesus say to us, "Greater works shall man do"? That just cancelled that theory out. Speak the desired outcome for what it is you want to happen. Confess only the word and omit the rest, for the rest to come to pass. This will cause unexpected hindrances from approaching your prayers. Expect immediate results. It shall come to pass!!!!!!!!! Remember, watch your mouth. I've told myself watch you tongue. "Think about what you are going to speak before you speak it." Words are like rockets; they will be launched into eternity for years to come. What type of fruit will you produce with your words? This is definitely for me (smile). Jesus said to Lazarus "come forth" and it was; his words created an awesome anointing to cause the dead corpse to rise. That resurrection power is available today—YES, in this season; YES, in this hour. I believe we are going to experience the greatest miracles that have already happened; however, I know we will have a chance to experience that for ourselves. Are you ready for your miracle? Receive the blessing by faith. The principle of the tithe will always produce the promise according to Malachi 3. The tithe is holy; you can stand on the devil not devouring your seed, because God promised that everything after the first tenth of obedience will be protected. Guess what? Saints of God we win...In Jesus' Name. No one wants to work in a field and in the end produce a field of nothing. NO. This is the same theory that God has instructed every born-again believer to operate in. Watch God blow on your tenth or tithe. I've seen too many times God protect my family's home that could have been foreclosed on. I remember when we had fallen behind on our mortgage payment, and the Holy Spirit had instructed that I go home. I was at my place of business and I heard "GO HOME NOW"????????

I thought okay, I'm not sure what this means but God, I will obey. The phone rang and I answered of course; yes, it was the mortgage company, and she said that at that moment she was minutes from walking our file to start the foreclosure proceeding. One thing that I learned is that once that starts, there is no turning back. God's grace and mercy showed himself strong once again. We were spared from the sting of foreclosure. Some families are not so fortunate; that is why I'm writing this book. Listen to the voice of the shepherd, and you know what he will direct the path's reference. The mortgage person allowed me to work out payment options, and God intervened on our behalf. That is the miraculous favor of God. Had I not obeyed the voice of the Lord, who knows what would have happened. Grace protected our property. Decree favor over our finances and life daily. Speak the word, apply pressure to the word. It will produce every time. God is awesome. Don't ever let anyone talk you out of what God wants you to do. Begin to ask God to reveal secret wisdom that you know not of. People divinely connected to you will be an awesome blessing. These would be the cheerleaders of your life. Also, be willing to be reproved in love. Real people won't always tell you what you want to hear. There are moments when it will not be so great, but remember that God will perfect everything in you that concerns him. **Blessing Blockers** are sent to destroy your purpose and destiny. Stay clear of these people unless God has instructed you that they are your assignment. Negative energy tends to drain you from being all that God has called you to be. The Bible declares you will know them by the fruit that they bear. Test the spirit by the spirit to see if they be of God. Be confident that God will always lift up a hedge of protection to those of his own. No harm will come near thy dwelling place Psalms 91.

There are people that God will put in your life that should be there to help you reach your fullest potential. Character is a great essential; you must know who you are in God. What is character? *Character* is defined how your habits, motives, and thoughts related to morality. In 1 Samuel 1 Hannah vowed to give her child back unto the Lord. Her character implicated that her word was bond. Character revealed her truthfulness. We see she made a promise to God that if he would bless her with a child, she would dedicate him back to God . Hannah executed loyalty to her word, predestined before the promise of her male child was conceived. Corrupt character would have opposed all of these traits, such as, honesty, and integrity. . Let your yes be yes and your no be no. People that are on your team will come forth. God have instructed those appointed as an assignment to you will, obey, and do it with gratitude. Prayer: Lord Jesus, I pray for those doors of opportunity that you allow to open to extend open. Thank you for power being available to see those people that you have ordained to be a blessing to me. We cancel out any jealous spirits that will try to abort our destiny. In Jesus name, Amen. Daily dispatch the angels of the heavenly hosts to go before you. Ask the Holy Spirit to guide you and order your footsteps; this will activate purpose-driven potential to become manifested in the earth realm. Watch Jesus move! Always remain in an attitude of gratefulness; no matter the circumstances, keep your joy. The joy of the Lord is your strength. Positive confessions will proceed from your mouth. Decree only the word. Focus your thoughts on a desired expectancy. Everything that you need is in the word of God. Search scriptures concerning the **expected end** that you desired to come. Pray always in faith. If it's healing, deliverance, finances, family, it's available in the word of God. Prayer will annihilate the enemy's weapons from forming; every day in faith, press, pursue, and dream into your next dispensation of your new next level of destiny. Fasting Mark 9:29 this too will render the enemy powerless in the earth realm. Jesus told his disciples to cast the devil out, and they pondered why they couldn't. Jesus replied that this one comes out only through fasting and prayer. Pray constantly without ceasing. Remain focused even through adversity!

Fasting allows you supernatural power that is available for every believer. Be bold in your pursuit; know that you can take the world by the power of the Holy Spirit. Remember the greater one is working on the inside of you. Tap into this anointing that will destroy any assignment that the enemy has tried to place on you. Amen. Also, be aware that you have to choose your battles wisely. It's not for us to fight every battle that comes our way 2 Chronicles 20:15. The battle belongs to the Lord. Fight the good fight of faith with the sword of the spirit. Oftentimes Christians are busy magnifying satan; notice I did not capitalize the *s* of satan because he is nothing. He doesn't have any jurisdiction over the children of God. Put this thought to flight. Give God the highest praise.... Forevermore God is almighty, ever present, omnipresent, ever knowing. He knows what's best. Ask the Holy Spirit to reveal when you need to intervene, or stand back and let God intervene. Pray that God will dispose of any ungodly relationships that are not of God; I called this "**The Blessing Blocker Factor.**" Stay away from **dream stealers**— those people that don't know who they are in God. Pray for them and move on. Life is so awesome. Receive today all that Jehovah Jireh has for you. You have to take a stand for righteousness. People will not always agree with your vision.

Note: God has placed that vision inside of you; NO wonder people will look peculiar when you tell them, "I'm going to own a fabulous yacht," or something of that nature. God did not show them your vision; he placed that dream on the inside of you. We all have our personal dreams. Today if you have lost your dream, begin to **DREAM AGAIN**.... Prayer: Father, somewhere along this road called life I have stop dreaming; please place the thing that I held onto back inside of me—my spirit and soul. Thank you, Father, that the best is still yet to come. In Jesus' Name, Amen. Come on, let's dream together—I'm cheering for you.... Go for it and don't look back...look to the future. Your tongue is a pen of a ready writer. Create your place of purpose with your mouth. Speak the word with your mouth. Never take the pressure off of the spoken word of God. Decree the end by what you confess with your mouth. Meditate daily on where you will envision yourself in the future. Write your vision and make it plain on tablets Habakkuk 2:2. Place pictures of tangible things that you can visually see every day. Something happens when you are able to lay your eyes on that prize that you are believing for. Create a dream board and make it a fun project as they manifest; in the natural you can celebrate the goodness of the Lord. Dream, dream, dream, dream, but while you're dreaming believe that it shall surely come to pass, because God's words are true. Also, remember to find a Mentor who is already walking in the dream. They can be your life coach. These are for sure people who are equipped to help you birth that baby. You will not abort the promise that has been conceived. This baby will be born. Will labor pains be involved? This means it is not going to be peaches and cream every day. Jesus said, take on my yoke, for it is easy. That being said, do not do this in your own might. Friends, the good news is you win in the end. That is exciting.... Prayer: Lord Jesus, thank you for giving me the desire to go forth in you. In my times of despair, in my trials of life that will surely come, I thank you that you will be my comforter that will never leave me or forsake me. I look forward to my new level in you. Thank you, Lord, for loving me. Amen. Ask God to reveal to you who you are to be associated with in this season of your life. Remember: guard your circle of influence. You might have to distance yourself in this place. But at this time of your life, you must guard yourself. Because remember, you want to have positive energy being reigned in your elements. Negative energy will only deplete what God is working in your life for your good 1 John 1:2. So as I say at times, cut them off! **The dream stealers.** Pray for them and move around. There were moments in my life when my family thought I was losing my mind, and I would always try to explain why I didn't go to the party or why I didn't go here or there. Then one day I realized wait a minute—I am not going to justify why I am not associating with certain people. The truth is, I did not even understand it. NOW I do. God was processing me. You say *processing*? Exactly. You see, I had to go through the school called Loneliness, but how many of you know this is when God shows himself to be LORD over your entire being? This was really when I experienced my greatest times of intimacy. God was placing things inside of my spirit that have now given Birth to this book. You see, one of my spiritual mothers once told me, "Baby, you are not going through for you, but for someone else." At that time I was only a babe in the Lord. Now looking back, it makes perfect sense now. How can you testify if you've never had adversity? The Bible says that we are overcomers by the words of our testimony. So as they say, "Go on through!" You will come out on the other side with a victorious shout of victory. Note that the greater the trail, the greater the Anointing. It comes with a price. Will you go through? Jesus died on the cross for our sins. I have confidence in this; we can sustain any hard trial that comes if you can only have endurance. *Endurance* means the ability to continue or last. There are times that you won't always feel like praying; there are moments when the Holy Spirit might instruct you to get up and intercede for someone. How many of you know that the spirit, wants to commune or fellowship with us, but often times the flesh nature will want to remain in bed. Procrastination is one of Satan's weapons that he uses against The Body of Christ; there is nothing new. If you think about it, there is nothing that he has not already tricked us with. He's the deceiver. What do you mean? Tap into and study how your life has been in the past. Maybe it's weariness in your body, strife in the home, confusion in the workplace. Disobedient children. Sexual sin. (Not married) Analyze these important areas and be careful to guard this; this will surely minimize the spiritual warfare that sometimes we tend to bring upon ourselves. Stay focused and know that he has already been defeated. You win in Jesus' name. Study daily to show yourself approved. Make this a vital part of your everyday life. No excuses; remember about the "firstfruits." What you do in the first part of the morning will govern the rest of your day. I believe when you press in to make God, Lord of your day every day, he is faithful to see us through any test or trial Satan might have to annihilate God's plan, but it will not prosper. This is a biblical principle, When we study First fruits Proverbs 3:9 "Honor the Lord with your wealth with the fruits of all of your crops, then your barn will be filled to overflowing and your vats will brim over with new wine." This is increase.... Pray, Pray, Pray to go into the Promised Land.

POSSESS THE LAND

WHERE ARE THE Joshua's and Caleb's? We must begin to rise and go into the enemy's camp and possess the land of the giants. What is possession? *Webster's* defines it as "to have as property, own." How on point is this definition? Oftentimes the enemy will tell you, "Oh don't go over there, it's not worth it." Don't believe the lies of the enemy. You know the story they were the ones that went in and said, "How can we go in, it's too hard for us to conquer" Joshua 1:16? But God will give you all of the spiritual tools you need to receive the goods of the promise. Resist the hindering spirits that will come to distract the promise. There will be people, sometimes those with whom you have a close relationship, that will tell you that you can't achieve your dreams. These are the **blessing blockers** that were shared previously. Remember, God gave you the vision, so don't be quick to release your destiny in a casual conversation; ask God to reveal who, what, when, and why in the season to embark this to the desired persons who are a part of this season in your life. Remember, this is your baby (**your dream**) so protect it. I believe in my own life. I have always been a dreamer; as a little girl my mother would say: Bridgett, we are poor, baby; I can't get this or that. I would reply, "Mama, you might be poor, but I'M NOT." What great faith for a child that was only five. I've always been a dreamer and would go for it. The very least that could happen would be if it failed and I could say I tried. I owned my first salon at twenty-one. Entrepreneur at a young age. I'll never forget that I worked for this lady that had a salon; it was small and my business flourished so expeditiously she began to make me feel uncomfortable, because the truth is I had more clientele than she did. One day I said I have to step out of faith and have my own. No one in my family was an entrepreneur that I knew of, but I felt in my spirit that the time was at hand. I bought used equipment, did not tell anyone, and launched Hairniques of Houston. I believe I had it to-gether in about a month. That is the timing of God: everything fell into place. Once I was ready to move on from this owner's salon, I thanked her for opening her doors to me, providing an opportunity for me to soar. Once I revealed to her that I was opening my own salon, she didn't say "Good Luck, God bless you," she said. "Yes, your volume here at my Salon is too Much." As a young woman that crushed my spirit. I went home, thought about it, released it to God, and I prayed for her and quickly made my exit from that place. Needless to say, she was not open for a long time after that. Be careful how you embrace people. What really disturbed me about this woman was she was a SO-CALLED Christian. But she did not walk in Love. I promised myself that I would not treat people or em-ployees the way I was treated. Maybe that's why God allowed me to go through those trials, so when my time came and it did, I would be a better Salon owner and not a Hater of others success. That taught me a valuable lesson about people who claimed to have Jesus as Lord of their life. I'm interested in the fruit that they bear. Prayer: Father, as I launch out into the deep, help me to look to the hills from which cometh my help and receive the instruction that you have graciously given to your children. I dispatch the angels to go in and begin to pave the way before we enter the land that is flowing with milk and honey. Define *possession*: it is defined as to have as property, own. God wants us to have a harvest of properties. For those who need finances, write out a plan to execute, a strategy to possess. This could mean clearing up credit issues. God will require that you be a good steward over that which he has already blessed you with (Joshua 1–6). Be strong and courageous. This simply means dig your heels in for the fight. Be rooted in the assignment that you will conquer. Because you will lead these people to inheritance the land I swore to their forefathers. To give the People of God this is our promise; we have a right to our inherited portion, so that the earth must yield and hearken to the commands of this word In Jesus' Name. Be careful to obey all that is written in it. Do not turn from it to the right or to the left so that you will be successful wherever you go. This is why it is so important to obey the voice of the Lord. The mysteries will be released through the spoken word. We must slow down so we can hear. Don't allow the enemy to get you too busy doing this or that. Stay Focused. Having a balance in your life will bring the promise in Proverbs 11:1. It is God's will for us to have Dominion over the Earth Realm Jeremiah 1:5. Before I formed you in your mother's womb, I knew you. He has set you apart for such a time as this. Yesterday was the greatest upset that American History has seen in a long time. Barack Obama was elected on November 4, 2008 of the United States of America. No matter what candidate of your choice was, History was made. God said before he was born, he called him a Prophet unto this nation. We pray that the bipartisanship can be mended, and they can be on one accord in Jesus' name. We must pray for the formation of his cabinet. I believe that other people, be it for good or bad, can have an influence on you; this is why it's key that we prune out, or periodically take an inventory of people that are in your life, and prune out those people that are hindering you. In Jesus' name. Farmers that care for crops understand this principle: they must prune off the dead leaves each year because this could choke the roots from receiving the desired nutrients in the root area. Once this process is done, more fruit will be produced. On the other hand, holding onto branches, although they appear alive, can hinder what's to come on the next year's harvest. Who do you have in your life that needs to be purged or pruned? Take a self-inventory and release the baggage. Your future depends on your obedience. Be in the know that Satan will not hand this territory over without a fight. But saints of God, Jesus has given us our spiritual weapons to fight the good fight of faith. You will endure if you don't faint Deut. 6:18; Isaiah 1:19. Dear God: I thank you that you have already created our path to go into the land flowing with milk and honey; we take authority over hindering spirits that may try to block our destination. We call you out; no weapon that tries to form will manifest or defeat our assignments. We will possess In Jesus' Name. Also, know that you have been appointed to be chief intercessor for your community at large. It is no accident that you live where you do. Pray for your neighborhood daily. Your prayers will make a major impact on crime, violence, peace, etc. So be persistent and stay alert at all times. If the Holy Spirit tells you to fast or get up to pray, be obedient; you don't know what is happening in the spirit realm, and you can intercept Satan's radar of evil by hearing the voice of the Lord. Amen. Ask God to bring you people of likeness or similarity into your circle. You want to run with the eagles. Visionary. I read once in an article that you don't want to always be the smartest in your circle. If you are, pray that God will send you a mentor into your life that will challenge you to come up higher. This is for me also. I like to be around bright, smart, sharp, articulate people. That anointing of knowledge will drop deeper on you, and you will begin to really see yourself soar. Pray daily that God will order your steps. The word declares that the good steps of a man are ordered by the Lord! Righteousness must be present forever for the promises to take dominion. Repent of any sin and receive all that is for you. We are heirs and joint-heirs with Christ. You are a royal priesthood. Conquer all and walk in Your dominion. In Genesis 1 God said "Let there be light" and light was so. Create your destiny with the power of the word of God. Can you imagine the authority that is released in the natural when you exercise your faith with your tongue? Open up the word and search the scriptures concerning any area in your life that needs prayer. Attack this with everything that is inside of you. God promises that it will not return void. I encourage those people of faith to speak what God says and know you will bat a 100 each time, because we are applying the biblical truths and you will see results. Be diligent in your pursuit. Apply pressure; don't stop pressing until you have tangibly manifested the promise in your life.

STANDING IN THE
STAND FOR DESTINY

YOU SAY, "PASTOR B, what exactly does this mean?" Standing in the Stand for Destiny no matter what obstacles come your way, you are persuaded that you will take this stand. You will be planted according to Psalms 1 like a tree on the river. When the storms of life come to try and blow us away, we are fully persuaded that we shall be unmovable, unshakable to declare to the gates of hell, "I will not give up my inheritance." We are entitled to everything that is your birthright. In the Old Testament, the Bible declared that the firstborn would have a greater anointing or blessing. Reference Genesis 27:Jacob deceived his father and stole his brother Esau's birthright. Satan knows that he cannot take anything from you if in fact this would be a violation of your covenant with God. Reference to when Jesus went to Hell and took back the keys from Lucifer.

Revelation 20:1-2 Saints of God, Satan has already been defeated. You don't have to fight someone that has been overthrown. But why as believers have we developed this wrong way of thinking concerning our covenant? Because of possible traditions, religions, cultures, or other various reasons. People sometimes develop habits, and if you have been bound in that mindset for years, this could alter your results that have not produced. Be strong and courageous Joshua 1:5. Come boldly to the throne of Grace to receive mercy. He did not say come with a pitiful plea to receive—no. Use power when you approach the throne. Note: the prayer of repentance; is vital in this approach, sin will separate us from God and sometimes this will stagnate our prayer petition. This is another trick of the enemy: Satan knows if you give over to sin, he wins. The good news is there are new Mercies every day Lamentations 3:22. Be sure to confess or renounce any sin and let's take this kingdom, for our time is at hand to declare the goodness of the Lord to ALL creation. Also, to activate this power you must believe by faith that you are free. If you sin, repent and move on. Forgive yourself and you are free. Free by faith, not by works. People are not allowing themselves to receive God's forgiveness because they don't think they are worthy. How many of you know God is merciful, he Loves you, and like Israel Houghton says, "He is not mad at you, he is madly in Love with you." I love that nothing could be further from the truth. Prayer: Lord, I repent of wrong mindsets and receive your grace and mercy this day and forevermore. Satan will no longer bind me to contrary thinking against the knowledge of God. Every stronghold that is trying to attack my mind, loose me now and let me go. In Jesus' name. I embrace this new way of thinking; give us the mind of Christ in Jesus' name... Amen. Develop a lifestyle of Prayer. Pray daily Genesis 30:1. Praying will unlock God's instruction that God will guide you to do. Another key that is vital in disarming the weapon of spiritual warfare. Set ambushments to annihilate the enemy's weapons 1 Chronicles 14:10–14. God will give you a strategic plan to help you execute the plan of the evil one. Never go into battle without a plan of action. Never go into battle without Fasting. Spiritual weapons are to be used at all times Ephesians 6:11–18. Spiritual weapons, for example, are praying in you heavenly tongues, fasting, and unforgiveness.The enemy will try his best to get you to abort God's blessings of provision from coming into your life. You must fight with the good fight of faith. Moreover, people will also try to cause distractions to get you blocked. Psalm 1. Faith will create a window for destiny to come into your life. Faith also will **UNLOCK** locked doors that have been shut, which will now become ajar(OPEN) because of this revelation. Fear will paralyze; Faith will Realize that yes, I too can have all that are my promises. Faith will allow you to walk through doors that most people are afraid to walk through. Don't allow your **MIND** to talk you **OUT** of the very thing you have been believing God for; step into your next level of dispensation. Yes you can…. Just Do It. God will not let you fall; his loving arms of shielded embrace will be there. Remember, you cannot do this in your **OWN** strength; invite the Holy Spirit to partner with you and all of your quests in this Journey; you will see it will be so much easier doing it **GOD'S WAY**. Always use your spiritual weapons to diffuse the enemies' strategic assignment against your destiny Ephesians 6:11–18. The enemy will try to get you to abort your destiny in your life. We must fight the good fight of faith. Remember: no matter how the attacks come, NEVER QUIT as victory is at hand…. Breakthrough is here.... Press, Press, Press. People will try, and I repeat try, to come against you Psalms 3:1. Let the naysayers and people of limited thinking talk. Never get into the debates to try to prove your points. Don't spend negative energy trying to persuade someone who really doesn't have your best interest at heart. Use negative stimulus to drive you. I remember not long ago at a salon that I worked at, there was talk going on with people who thought they knew me but really didn't know talking. Points like "she calls herself a preacher." When I heard that I laughed; you see that was petty—I don't have to validate who I am; God called me in 1998. That was all she wrote on that point. My point, people of God, is my dad once said, "Long as you're being talked about, that's a good thing." Bless his soul, Daddy went to be with the Lord in 2005; he would say, "You get concerned when people stop talking." I didn't really know what that meant; boy do I ever now. Great revelation of wisdom had spoken. You see, no one can stop your anointing. Ignore the comments, gossip, naysayers and keep your head high. This will cause you to lose sight of the Promised Land. Pray for the backbiters and watch God bless you like you've never seen. Fear will cancel out faith. What is fear? It is, simply put, False Evidence Appearing Real. It looks one way. But children of God, that is an illusion. Don't allow yourself to get trapped with the What If Question. What if this happens? What if that happens? The truth is that is Satan toiling with your imagination. The worst could not possibly take place. Would it not be a tragedy to allow your dreams to go in vain with a vain imagination? We must conquer the stronghold in our minds called self. There are those who are their own worst enemy. It's a true statement. This is why you must renew your mind daily to cast down vain imaginations. Be guarded and watch the things that you entertain on television or the eye gate; be mindful of your ear gate—be careful what you listen to. You don't want ungodly garbage to enter your spirit man. Protect yourself as you would your own child. This is vital in your stand for destiny.

WALKING WITH DESTINY, OBTAINING FAVOR GOD'S WAY

HAVING A HEART of a Servant.... In today's society, people have developed an attitude of not wanting to serve. We have become so spoiled and somewhat selfish for our own good. This very component is missing. What can we do as the body of Christ to get back into God's way of doing things? Not our way But God's way. He left us with a manual for life—it is called the Bible. Oftentimes we want to delete certain things that are written because of the conviction. Servanthood is vital Psalms 90:16, 17; Ephesians 6:5, 6. In the book of Ruth we see the true epitome of servanthood. Ruth was a noblewoman. She had great discernment and influence. Her mother-in-law Naomi had the ability to foresee a greater revelation of life's events because of previous life experiences. She was able to share the rough roads that she had to journey upon. Ruth understood servanthood in her. Let me serve, glean, and grab a wealth of knowledge from someone who has lived before me. Who would not welcome someone that has gone the distance to see you? Know that I can see the anointing operating in this person's life. Although in the book of Ruth, Naomi told her, "Leave me and go back to your country." She understood that her blessing was tied to Naomi, and she needed to walk with her on this road to get to her place called THERE.... You must gain wisdom, knowledge, and understanding. How can we gain destiny if we don't have revelation or wisdom on how to obtain it? Prayer: Father, help me to understand my pathway that you are taking me on. Those people that you have appointed to help me on this journey, allow them to present themselves to me. I know this road called life will not always be easy, but I look forward to a greater richness in you. In Jesus' Name. Ruth walked into riches because of obedience; she heard the voice of God. Remember: Naomi told her to go back, Destiny said stay with Naomi. She came face to face upon her approach of hearing the voice of the Lord. Ruth was also a noble woman. I would say a woman of courage, wisdom, knowledge, and understanding. In Mike Murdock's book *The Leadership Secrets of Jesus*, he quotes that you must respect those people who are in Authority over you. This is a biblical principle and a natural principle as well. Your success will depend on it. Honor those who have lived before you; they possess a wealth of knowledge. This was in fact what Naomi said; to her mother-in-law she knew that wealth of experiences would be a vital role in her success to meet her season of wealth via her husband Boaz. Naomi respected the covering of this valuable relationship. Disconnect from those people who are not going in the same direction as you. This will only delay God's perfect plan for your life. Destiny will arrive upon seeking this principle ingredient. What is *destiny?* It is defined as the outcome of fate that is bound to come. *Webster's* also gives the definition as "the power which is believed to decide the course of events in advance." Wow, that is powerful. Inquire about your calling from the Lord God. That factor is Wisdom. In the book of James, it says "he that lacks wisdom let him ask." This tells me when you pray and you are pursuing a desired goal, go to God and inquire wisdom. Listen and follow the leading of the Holy Spirit; he will lead you down the correct pathway. Wisdom will also come through fasting and prayer. It's amazing to me the times when I would go on a fast, I could hear the voice of the Lord so clearly; yielding my spirit to the things of God and telling my flesh to shut up takes diligence. Remember: stay on course; the enemy will use these times to tempt you. Remember when Jesus was on the fast in the wilderness and Satan came to tempt him. Matthew 4:1-11. After seeking the face of wisdom, you must encounter understanding. Understanding is the ability to relate to any given subject. One has to also obtain revelation about a topic. After you have developed understanding , now we know how to attack any area of uncertainty. After this is applied to your life, there is nothing one can do to stop this flow from success. Success is inevitable; stay on point and meditate at this level even more. This will ensure that this drops down in your spirit. The enemy doesn't care about you knowing too much, but to gain understanding this element is vital to your success. This will disarm his tactics; now we are going into momentum. *Momentum* is defined as "the force of the ability of an object to move." As believers, we have to have a mindset to excel with motion. Acceleration is at hand. Go Forth. Prayer: Father, I thank you for understanding in the things that are set before me. Grant me the understanding of my circumstances. Father, I refuse to be ignorant in my quest for destiny. No longer will I be bound by Satan's tactics. We are free and welcome this time to seek you, Father; God, grant me divine understanding so I may prosper in everything I set my hand to (1 John 3). Thank God for freedom and liberty. Amen.

PURPOSE

WHY ARE YOU here? Why were you even born? I know this seems strange, but how many of us know those individuals that are walking through life from day to day? Not maximizing their callings and giftings. What a tragedy. My prayer in writing this book is to help someone discover their passion and reach for the stars. First you must always acknowledge God put himself CEO over everything that belongs to you. It doesn't belong to us; he wants us to be great Stewards over what he has already blessed us with (see Servanthood and Stewardship chapter for more insight on this topic). Furthermore, understand what Jeremiah was talking about when God told him, "before you were formed in your mother's womb I knew you" Jeremiah 1:5. God has spoken destiny into all of our lives. This makes the distinction that the word is clear we are born with Destiny. I saw on a talk show where the group Destiny's Child was given through the scripture. Beyonce's mother indicated that one day she was reading the Bible and the word *Destiny* leaped from the page. I believe that was a rhema word that God had placed on the inside of her. Not only that, but each time someone said the name Destiny's Child they were proclaiming their Destiny. That is awesome. Friends, God is no respecter of persons; what he does for one he will do for another. I named my second child, first daughter, London; somehow I knew when she was in my womb she will be famous one day, and she will be known all around the world. She is an aspiring Singer, Actress, Dancer, and Songwriter. Look out—she shall walk in all that God has destined her to be for his kingdom, and it's time to walk into our next dominion of blessings and anointings. Be strong, Be vigilant, Walk in authority, Be bold, and let's take this back for the Glory of Our Lord and Savior. Prayer: Father, I thank you that you have created greatness inside of this vessel that is praying this prayer right now. Let us discover untapped potential that is inside of us. We bind the spirit of fear over us. Fear has no place in our lives. We put you under our feet now In Jesus' Name. We thank you, Jesus, for giving us this opportunity to seize this moment; we will hold fast to our confessions without wavering and doubts in our hearts. This too shall come to pass In Jesus' Name. It *is* vital that we take out the time to discover the purpose of our Destiny. How could you do this? Let's see if the Holy Spirit will lead us…. Let's call this "The Blueprint to My Success." First you need to ask yourself what it is that I enjoy doing. By this I mean, what are you passionate about? Like if you could do this gift without pay, that would be fine. That's a great start. For me when I was a little girl, I knew my area of field would be beauty related because I enjoyed the thought of Glamour and Prestige…. I enjoyed wearing apparel and applying makeup. Even as a child I valued shoes, clothing, dolls, etc.

My mother discovered something when I was around five. She would always tell me, "Bridgett, I think you should be a beautician." I thought, what was that?... As life progressed, I discovered my passion in The Arts and Beauty Industry. I became an Entrepreneur at the age of 21 (working for myself). Owner of my first salon at such a young age. My mother would always say to me, "Bridgett, you don't like taking orders, I think you should work for yourself," and you know I discovered quickly she was right. I don't have those challenges anymore; you see, God had to teach me the importance of protocol. Submitting to authority. To become a great success, one must first learn how to humbly submit to leadership. After this is mastered, you are ready for Kingdom Promotion. Note: this is a process, so be patient in this transitional time. God is perfecting everything in you which concerns him. At this time, you must be aware of the people that you are connected to. Don't allow toxic relationships to clog up your line. Those barriers of toxicity will stifle the growth that the Holy Spirit is trying to impart. This is critical; it is important every day for you to ask the Holy Spirit to guide you and to order your steps. I firmly believe that you must be at the place of Grace that Jesus will have you to be. Stop, Listen, and Obey what the Spirit is telling you. This could also mean cutting away people that you have been linked to for years. Please don't try to be overanalytical; just move with the cloud. Your blessing is tied with the obedience. Wake up each day thanking God for all he has done. Spend as much intimate time with The Father as you can.

Vast in his presence daily; there should be a dedicated place in your home that you can meet God. This is your sanctuary!!!!! Cleanse your environment of demonic activity. Remember, light and darkness cannot dwell together—one will cancel out the other. So cleanse your environment of evil forces, as the Holy Spirit gives you utterance. I will explain that later in another chapter. What is intimacy is defined as resulting from firsthand knowledge.... Jesus wants to reveal to each and everyone of us firsthand knowledge.... I call this "Straight from The Throne Room"...Up Close and Personal. That is the kind of God we serve; he wants us to have the best.... This will require persistence and diligence to be in a position to receive what thus says the Lord Psalms 119–125. How can you achieve this knowledge?... How can you know Good versus Evil if you do not allow this quality time to spend with God? For example, in the natural a mother who has birthed her children knows each and every one of them. She can tell you about their character. She knows detail after detail the things of her children. She knows the ones that may need a little more nurturing, versus the one who may be strong by nature. The child that is very independent perhaps are more self-sufficient, more motivated. Essentially, many parents realize the important values that each of the siblings need. I think about my own children. There is Cedric: he's opinionated, chief, knows what he wants, but I know he seems as though he has it all together with the language he says. However, he's the one who needs encouraging on.... He needs extra reinforcement.... There is London; she has it together. Even as a little baby, she walked before she was nine months.... She's very secure and knows what she wants, knows how to make it happen. At home she is like the mother hen; even when she was three the babysitter would always tell me, "I don't think you should pay me." London would help her keep the other children. Even now she adores little ones.... Alec, he is the opposite; he's independent in a different way. He's quiet; even in school his teacher tells us about how awesome he is in school. He makes friends very easily. He loves to build things with his hands. The baby Mirren—my baby girl, she is she feisty, I clearly see a lot of my traits in her. She knows how to get what she wants. She's a tough cookie. But she is very lovable. She too is like London, very much in control.... Our children, I believe, are our greatest assets, and we must pray continuously for them to become all that God would have them to be. Prayer: Lord Jesus, help us to commit to being great parents to our children. Father, you said in your word that children are your precious gift from you. Help us to shape them into being ambassadors for the kingdom of God. We thank you that they are blessed and everything they do will prosper and bring Glory and Honor to you.

Servanthood &
Stewardship:
Principles of the Seed

What Is Stewardship? A person who manages the property or finances… Genesis 14–7; Genesis 1;

Genesis 26:4, 5. Read 5 first, then 4. Must have a giving mindset; never give out of obligation.

Remember God does not need our money; it all belongs to him. He owns a cattle of a thousand hills Malachi 3:5–12; Luke 19:12. God will bless us according to our stewardship. We are required to govern our resources that he has provided us with…. Do not eat your seed or store it. In the book of Luke, Jesus called him a wicked servant. Pray about everything; follow the leading of the Holy Ghost. Always go with your gut instinct. There are obedient rewards for Servanthood 2 Corinthians 9:5–8; Job 42–12 . Pray about your giving. Where to sow? Mark 4:8. "This is a Rich Soil Ministry." Good Fruit Will Bear from This Ministry. We are on different levels of giving. That does not mean we don't love God the same. We simply have different levels of faith. So we will all have different harvesting appearing in our lives on different levels. Be encouraged to be faithful in your giving. Purpose-Driven giving, you ask? Purpose-driven giving is to put our individual seeds dispatched into eternity to produce a harvest right now. Stay on your individual plan of action that the Holy Spirit gives you. Be diligent and steadfast in your giving; God will reward you for your level of obedience.

Discerning the
Voice of God

Jonah knew what this meant. He heard the voice of the Lord clearly, but out of rebellion he chose to ignore the voice of God. God instructed that he go to Nineveh but he insisted on sailing to Tarshish; this was not God's will for him. Let's look at parenting for a moment. How can a person discern their child's voice? This comes through close intimacy and relationship. A mother, for instance, could be in a park with 100 other little voices, but at the sound of her little one's cry, would instantly be heard amongst the rest. Why? Because of relationship, bonding, and nurturing.... This is the same thing that the Father wants from us. He longs for us to spend time with him. You say, well how can I hear God's voice? Easy: through intimacy. How will you know Good versus Evil if you don't spend one-on-one with him? This comes through fasting Matthew 6:16–20. You must also have a yielded spirit. Being careful to always pray with supplications and thanksgiving, giving thanks for all that the Father has done. Having a heart for the kingdom. Knowing that it is not "About Me." Lose the mentality of the "I, I, I" syndrome—don't be selfish. Always be willing to lend a hand to service. It is more a blessing to give than to receive Acts 20:35. Fasting will unlock the hidden mysteries of the Father. You will begin to discover things that ordinarily would not have been discovered. The spirit is sharpened at this time. Also, the onsets of attacks become minimized through prayer Mark 9:29. Make a conscious decision to spend quality time; I encourage those who can to start the day early before the house wakes up. Remember what is done first so that the firstfruits will govern how your day will be. I believe if you allow that time early in the day, God will make up the time to you…. It's been proven in my life time after time. Praying in the spirit will help to sharpen your discernment. The Bible declares that during times when as believers we just don't know what to pray for or about, these are the times to pray in the Holy Ghost or your heavenly language. If you have not received this gift , it is free to all who wants to receive it. Prayer: Father I desire to go higher in my worship with you, bless me to receive this gift that is available with the evidence of speaking in an unknown tongue. In Jesus name Amen 1 Cor 14:14-15 During times of warfare is the time to pray without ceasing; you MUST build your spirit man up. Don't let up until the victory is conquered. And even then, don't develop a relaxed spirit; stay on guard at all times. I always like to say, "Don't wait for the battle to begin to get suited up with the armor." Like Ernest would often say, "Stay ready so you don't have to get ready!"

How awesome is that? Praise, Praise, Praise. Acts 16: 25-34 Paul and Silas gave the Lord a praise break at midnight. You want to give the devil an attack. I dare you to give God the Glory for All That He Has and Is Going to Do.

THY KINGDOM COME

As a believer in my earlier walk with the Lord, I was a very negative person by nature. I was always that kind of a person people would always tell me they wanted to be around. There were times when I could remember purposely being late because I needed to make a grand entrance to whatever event I was invited to. The truth was I had to ask myself, why do you feel a need to be late all of the time? The truth was I had my own insecurities going on inside of me. I had to deal with the root reason why I needed to be affirmed by others. You see, I had to learn quickly that people, places, or things will not complete my existence; only God could give me my true wholeness. I had to search deep into myself to know that I had insecurities going on. As I developed a relationship with God, I realized that he loves me, even with my imperfections; I needed to begin to become accountable for my actions. So as I began to walk with the Lord, little by little those little foxes that were trying to destroy my very existence began to disintegrate. I did not receive complete deliverance overnight. It was a process. So be patient; remember some of us have developed strongholds that have been in operation for a long time, so give yourself time. Confess to Jesus what it is you're battling with; find scriptures concerning what the issue could be. If it's unforgiveness, go to the word. It could be patience. Seek the word over whatever the situation is and apply biblical truths. You will render results because you have applied the word of knowledge over your battle. I could remember times when my feelings of anxiousness always tended to get the best of me. You see, for the kingdom to come on Earth, we have to begin to pull things from the Spirit Realm into the Natural. There is a process of God's Kingdom to Come to us on earth. The Kingdom Coming simply put is Goodness, Mercy, Grace, Blessings, Prosperity, Victory, Healing, All things Good. Thy Kingdom Come—wow; when the Spirit of the Lord told me "Thy Kingdom Come," I literally felt something hit the atmosphere. I began to seek God about the kingdom becoming visible here in the earth realm. Prosperity is a vital part of allowing the kingdom of God to manifest in our lives. How can we have the blessings—I mean MONEY—if we are barely making it ourselves? Let's face it: how are we going to be a witness for Christ if we are barely getting by? We must begin to condition our minds on kingdom blessings. I believe we must first change our thinking, begin to think positively. But you see, my friends, for this to happen one has to bring it out of the Spirit, we first must position our mindset to begin to ponder on kingdom principles. To change our way of thinking, we must think positively, even when things are not going so well. Stay in an attitude of gratefulness. God honors faith, not complaining.

How do we begin to start this? First, we must search the scriptures and begin to confess everything that needs to be pulled down. Demonic strongholds over ourselves as well as our loved ones. Prayer: Father, we bind satanic influences over ourselves and our family members (Note: call them out by name); we take authority over everything that is not like God. We pull down vain imaginations that will try to exalt themselves against the knowledge of Christ, bringing every thought CAPTIVE unto the obedience of Christ. Thy Kingdom will only come to those who are committed to the gospel. Seek ye first the kingdom of God and his righteousness, and all of these things will be added unto you. Know who you are in covenant with. How can we receive the Kingdom or Promises if we are not first born into his own? Romans 8–7; Acts 2–16. Begin to look through your eyes of faith and see yourself as royal priesthood adopted into the kingship of glory 1 Peter 2:9. Hallowed Be Thy Name Luke 6–38). When we reference the word *Hallowed what are we saying specifically?* The angels of the Lord hearkened to this word…Holy, Holy, Holy. It means also consecrated or sanctified. Child of God, the angels are waiting for us to dispatch them to go and get our stuff to bring consumers to you. Amen.

Let me say this is God's way of doing things. We must get this order of operation correct. Place the kingdom first and everything else will fall into place. This is a promise we can have faith in knowing that God will get involved in our plans. As a result, of our obedience we will see our plans succeed. There are often times that God will test us in seeing that we will be steadfast in our walk. I made up my mind a long time ago that I'm going all the way with God. Saints, this is the kind of attitude that we must have. No matter how the winds toss me to and fro, I will not be double-minded. I'm planted according to

Psalms 1 like a tree by the river. So no matter how things are looking in the natural, know that we have to be fully persuaded that we are not in this walk for only tangible things, but our soul is to be rescued so heaven will be our home. We will be sure of our eternal life in Christ Jesus. Salvation is key. Prayer: Lord Jesus, I ask you to come into my heart, wash me with your precious blood; I repent of my sins. Father, forgive me and cleanse me from all unrighteousness. Today I will accept you in my heart as my Lord and Savior. Note: If you have been delivered from any addictions or strongholds, use wisdom and remove yourself from negative environments that could create temptations in your life. Ask the Holy Spirit to remove negative people out of your life, and replace them with new accountable friends that will have your back. (IN PRAYER) Amen.

The Blessing Blockers

The Blessing Blockers, you say? What is this? Just what it is; these are The Pharisees dream stealers, dream killers, or we can simply say they are the haters. Not everyone will be excited about the blessing that is going on in your life. I have to present this book with balance. I will not just say, "Oh everything will be great; say this, turn around ten times, and everything will work out." That's nice but most likely will not produce anything. Pray in season as well as out. Toxic friendships will clog up the blessings flowing in your life. Remember, go where you will be appreciated and valued. You are to be a blessing whenever God sends you. Most of the blessing blockers are carnal-minded folks, just downright wicked... Romans 8:1–6. The Bible declares that to be carnal-minded is Death and Spirit-minded is life and peace.... OK, do the math. You choose. There cannot be any Spirit of Division over any of us Matthew 12–25. That's what I love about God; he is gentle and meek, and he will give us our own free will. He is such a gentleman. He will never force us to accept him, but who could turn this great reward away? Do not eat the bread of idleness. Stay focused on the task that is set before if you noticed you have gotten off course get back ON THE ROAD. Let's say you are the person that I am speaking of . It's not too late to turn from the wicked ways, repent, and ask God to remove the anger, malice, strife—whatever the issue might be that will take you outside of God's divine will. You are valuable in the eyesight of God; he has great work for you to do…. I'm sure if you have made it this far in this book, you have a great idea of the Divine Purpose for your life. Tap into this anointing; let the rivers of water begin to flow. We expect divine impartations of the Holy Ghost to reveal things that we know not of. Prayer: Father, I ask you to remove any bitterness, anger, malice, strife, envy. Anything that is defiling my relationship with you. I renounce past mistakes, hurts, failures, and I forgive not only others that I have offended, but I also forgive myself. Thank you, Father, for allowing me another chance to receive this grace and mercy. Amen. Remember Jesus loves you…. Don't allow the enemy to have the playground called The Mind anymore. It is done!!!!!! In Jesus' Name.

HAVING THE FAITH
IN THE PRESS...

IN THE BOOK of Matthew 6:30 Jesus is saying, **"Wherefore, if God so clothe the grass of the field, which today is, and tomorrow is cast into the oven, shall he not much more clothe you, O ye of little faith? Therefore take no thought saying what shall we eat?"** One thing we should be clear on: we are in a faith fight. The enemy knows that we will master our destiny with God on our side. However, we have to show the enemy that we will conquer him through our faith confessions. Remember, the greater one is working on the inside of you. It is imperative that we know that there are times when we will grow weary. But the word declares we shall reap if we faint NOT.... We will Win.... This is good news. We must know that Jesus is not moved by how we feel; he is moved by our level of faith. I remember in my walk with the Lord, there have been moments when I felt as though God had abandoned me. You see, the truth is he is always there to help us with our obstacles. We also have to commission the angels to go ahead of us and prepare the way. I believe our life will be more or less resistant if we begin to simplify our lives. Let's use the area of finances for a moment. How many of you know if you have no bills to be concerned with, that will be a great place to be in? Debt is a demon in itself, it robs many Christians of their joy. I've been depressed because I could not seem to see my way out of the financial snare called debt. In 2009, God revealed a word for the people, the Holy Spirit, said to live with SIMPLICITY. "Bridgett, tell my people to simplify their lives." This means do not try to be involved in everything that comes up. If you know it will rob you of one of your times with God, this intimacy with him is more important. How can we hear God if we are so busy? Note: this is a trick of the enemy to distract the very thing that God needs you to know for your life. Matthew 11:28: **"Come unto me, all ye that labour and are heavy laden, and I will give you rest."** We can rest in this scripture; Jesus is clear on us having a life that is balanced…. I apply this daily into my life, and saints of God this has made life more accommodating. Not saying that I don't have obstacles, but the trials are easier for me to recover from because of this basic principle. Simplicity works! This is not saying not to strive for your goals—this will help you achieve your goals because you have put away the weights that could try to easily entangle you into the web of despair. Let's take inventory. Do you have a lot of clutter in your home? This will be addressed later in another chapter. Clean your house spiritually and naturally. Jesus has already taken up the cross to every opposition. We cannot fight the good fight of faith in our flesh…. 2 Corinthians 10:3: **"For** though we walk in the flesh we do not war after the flesh." We have to fight with our spiritual weapons. 2 Corinthians 10:4: **"For our weapons of our warfare are not carnal, but mighty through God to the pulling down of strongholds."** The opposite of faith is fear. One will cancel out the other. Choose faith; don't allow the enemy to pollute your mind with negative thinking. It is necessary to renew your mind daily with prayer and meditation. Think on good things. Without faith we cannot please Our Father. We have to call those things that are not as though they are…. This is true; I can't tangibly see it so I will pull it out of the spiritual realm and take it by force in the natural. Satan never wants you to discover this untapped power that is on the inside of us. I PURPOSELY put pressure on this word until it is visibly manifested…. That is Powerful.

Receive this revelation and let's take back everything that the enemy has stolen from us. He must pay it back seven times. We must learn that we cannot allow ourselves to fight this battle in our flesh; know that this is a spiritual fight. You have to win this battle with spiritual weapons: fasting and seeking the face of the master.

"Recover All"

RECOVER IS DEFINED as "To get back after losing. A coming back to health, to regain to make up for as a loss. To get well. To restore oneself to balanced health. To make useful again." I announce to the Body of Christ we shall recover all that has been stolen from us. Our joy, peace, finances, family, unity, harmony, and you insert in this phrase _____ (whatever has been taken by the adversary). We declare that 2017 is mine in Jesus' name. This is not just a rhyme, this is a prophetic year. With this new presidential administration I believe change is here. I also believe that we should have his family daily in our prayers. We must pray for all of our leaders globally around the world. The scripture declares there will be peace in Jerusalem before Christ will return. Together we work on this end-time harvest. I'm confessing no longer will it be business as usual. America have to be patient with our current president Barack Obama and continue to undergird him. How can one continue to do things the same way and expect different results. This is insanity. No, we are seeking God for counsel, direction, clarity, wisdom, knowledge, and understanding. Prayer: Holy Spirit, grant us discernment of gaining heavenly insight on what it is we need to possess this land. We will heed to your voice and walk in pure obedience to do whatever it is you are instructing, even when we don't fully understand what it is you're saying. We will trust you at all times; we know with you on our side ALL IS WELL…In Jesus' Name, Amen. Now let's look at this scripture. Proverbs 13:20: **"He that walketh with wise men shall be wise, but a companion of fools shall be destroyed."** We can see we want to consult wise council. Ask the Holy Spirit to reveal to you a good mentor who can help you on your journey. You should never be the smartest one in the group. You need someone who can stretch you into your God-given potential. Hang around people that are going places; on the other hand, get with people who have obtained prosperity by doing it God's way. In the book of Samuel we see that the Amalekites had talked of stoning David; this brought great distress to David. Now we know that the people were frustrated in their despair. Let's look at what David did. He could have possibly abandoned the camp and fled elsewhere. But no, in 1 Samuel 30:8: **"And David enquired at the Lord saying, Shall I pursue after this troop? Shall I overtake them? And he answered him. Pursue: for thou shall surely overtake them and without fail recover all."** We must also be like David—never go into the enemy's camp not armed with your armor on. Notice David prayed before he executed. People of God, could it be that we are going ahead of God, not allowing him to give us the strategy on how to attack the enemy's plan to totally disarm Satan's tactics? We have the faith to know that God will bless us back with more than we had with the former things Joshua 3. In this chapter God is giving Joshua instructions about the Ark of the Covenant. Verse 7: **"And the Lord said unto Joshua, This day will I begin to magnify thee in the sight of Israel, that they may know that, as I was with Moses so I will be with thee."** WE must mature as Christians. Pass the test. We should go from faith to faith. Glory to Glory. If you examine your walk and you are around the same mountain as last year or even last week, realign yourself with the word. There may be some other root problems that need attention. Seek help… from your Pastor, or you may need some Deliverance. Let's examine in the book of Job about his recovery. We are all familiar with the story of Job and how his wife told him to curse God and die. Isn't that like some of us women? We are always running our mouths. I believe as women we must learn how to follow our husbands. I'm guilty; there have been times when the spirit of the Lord would reveal to me all of the things that I was finding wrong with my husband, and The Lord told me, "What about you take your eyes off of what Ernest is NOT doing and be thankful for what he did do?" I encourage those reading this book to list an inventory of all the things that are great qualities about your spouse. On blank sheets of paper and write the pros and cons. On the list write what is irritating you—or should I say "challenging you" (smile)—take them to God in prayer. Also examine your heart , to see any unresolved areas that need prayer. I've learned that it's good to communicate about what you need in your covenant partner, but if it's resulting in strife and confusion, then pray about it. Remember to search the scriptures over whatever it is and Hit the Nail on the Head. You see, when we pray we shall have results. Pray the word; it shall not return void. If you are married to an unsaved spouse, pray for your covenant partner and know that the Bible declares that the sanctified wife sanctifies the husband or vice versa. Just let your light shine and God will do the rest. Go to someone who is married with good fruit on their life and ask them to lift you up—this is an effective tool. What greater person to pray is one who has been there, done that—as I say, has plaques on the Wall for it! People that have walked in victory with a certain issue, I believe, have a greater anointing for whatever that may be to pray that person out of the hands of the enemy. They have defeated that stronghold. People who have experienced victories in specific areas of difficulty will be qualified to pray on your behalf. Why? Simply because they have overcome that tasks.

"Walking with Destiny, Obtaining Favor God's Way"

Having a heart of a servant Psalms 90:16, 17. **We can begin to look at the book of Ruth.** Ruth was a noble woman. One should be steadfast, persistent, tenacious. We must begin to respect those who are in authority over us. This means in the marketplace, ministry is taking a front seat to meet the demand of the needs of the people. No longer can we go from Sunday to Sunday before we can feel that refreshing. God has strategically placed people in key positions inside of corporate settings that are getting KINGDOM business handled. That is an awesome assignment. I remember when God gave me a two-year assignment at Tuscany Village Salons, and boy was that an assignment. But the truth of the matter is that God had poured his loving arms of grace and mercy over me. I was in the lion's den. I felt sometimes like God, I am out of here. I have met some amazing people who are now some of my dearest friends. Had I not obeyed God's instruction, who knows where I would be right now? I encourage you to allow the Holy Spirit to lead and guide into all truths. If he said it, he will grace you with the anointing that you need to get the job done. Never go in your own strength: the enemy will defeat you. But with God we know ALL things are possible. Ruth understood servanthood and stewardship. She served Naomi even after her sons were killed; she instructed her to depart and go back. Remember, God will never allow you to go backwards. She knew that her destiny was attached to the very bosom of Naomi. We understand by divine instructions, as her mother-in-law gave her instructions to go to the field and glean for food. She could have complained and said, "No, it's hot; why do I have to go? Can't we just wait for another day?" The Bible declares that she went consistently every day. It was not until she was noticed by Boaz. He was a very wealthy man. We see that Ruth was not a lazy woman; she had an assignment, and the first principle was to serve her mentor Naomi . Folks, there is an anointing in serving. Do not discount serving as some cheap escape. That could NOT be further from the truth. Naomi could have been a hater and said selfishly, "I'm not introducing her to Boaz." Everyone knew him in that day. He was loaded. I believe because of purification and sanctification that was in her heart, God allowed her to come face to face with destiny. This also shows the kind of character that Naomi had; she wanted the best for Ruth. Remember she was married to her son before, so she could have manipulated that. But she knew God's judgment would have been against her. My spiritual father, Dr. Hughes, told me recently, "Daughter, I expect you to do greater things than I; you see the student far surpasses the teacher." I was blessed by his wisdom. How could I possibly do what he has done? I feel that I haven't even begun to scratch the surface. A mentor in the wrong spirit would never admit to his protégé that he would pass him up, so to speak. I encourage you to begin to pray about your covering. You need to be under someone who can show you not only the good, but will be willing to rebuke in love, so you can be all that God will have you be for his Glory.

DILIGENCE WITH A MISSION

DILIGENCE IS DEFINED as "Hard, careful work; willingness or ability to work steadily and carefully. Plan." In order to execute this plan for our life to get this mission funded, we must begin to strategize our blessed plan of action for the glory of God. Attacks have tried to stagnate me as I was writing this book, but you know this is a very good chapter for me to talk about persistence. How bad do you want it? I often ask people, "How bad do you want it?" It's here for the takers, and you know the violent TAKE IT BY FORCE. You see, no one is going to give you anything, and the truth is it is so much better when you work for your success. While you are on this mission, have a game plan. How do you plan to master this mission? Have you researched it? Did you write it down according to Habakkuk 2:2? Did you make it a plan? Now let's look at the next step to this mission. Did you pray for the leading of the Holy Spirit on this mission? If so, write down while you are in prayer, what did he tell you? Wait on the green light. Please don't get anxious. Wait and be patient. I am a firm believer that what is for you, is for you. Next seek godly wisdom; I know you said you heard it, "ask God to give you wise council." In the scriptures it tells you that without wisdom, your plans will not be established Matthew 7–11. Let's look at the woman with the issue of blood. The scriptures said that she had been with this infirmity for over twelve years; can you imagine how weak she had to have been? I can use my sanctified imagination and infer that it started out as a thought, okay, Jesus is in town so I will make my way through the crowds. If I can just touch his garment, I know I will be made whole. She was that word PERSISTENT; she did not allow her current state to determine her destiny. She was probably thinking, I'm weak; you know she did not have a good life, just imagine being in that state. She took her eyes off of herself and looked to the hills. Her help cometh from the Lord. We know the end of the matter: she was indeed made whole. I admire her willingness to go against all odds. I'm sure she did not smell the best; that did not stop her. She touched the master and the Bible declared that she was made whole.

Divine Purpose with Manifested Power

Joseph was a man who had favor with God. Why was his brothers so jealous of him? Oftentimes people can see you in the blessings. Sometimes the spirit of jealousy will rise up over them because of their inferiority that they are battling with; the truth is it has nothing to do with you. This is an issue that they must get delivered from. We must begin to purposely unload the junk out of our trunks. His brothers could not see the blessing that this could have provided for them. I believe if you have one family member, to make it so that to speak to them the whole family is in. This was quite the contrary with Joseph; his brothers hated his very existence. Favor will take you places that money will not allow access. I call this "The Joseph Anointing." There was confusion in the camp as the spirit of jealousy had rose up. Strife, Malice, and Discord will block manifested power from flowing. What's preventing the blessing power and anointing from coming into visible manifestation? Resurrected power is available. We must do a daily self-check. A self-check is simply allowing the Holy Spirit to scan our spirit man to make sure that the fruits of the spirit are in order. What are the fruits. Love, Joy, Patience, Peace, Gentleness, and Self Control. David said, "Search me, Oh Lord, that I may have a clean heart." Do you love? Has someone offended you?… If you have unforgiveness, renounce any sin, known and unknown, and move forward. Secondly, to go to the next level in this self-check; you must first unload all of the junk mail in your inbox. How many of us have access to e-mail? Probably about 98% of us do. When you click to the inbox icon, there is also a junk mail. What is the junk mail?

Our junk mails are the things keeping us from a direct connection to God. For example, in Colossians 3:8 " **But now you also, put them all aside anger, wrath, malice ,slander, and filthy communication from your mouth**". What was Paul saying about this passage? What's in our life that is causing this confusion and tension? This will pollute our walk with the Lord. *Flow*: it's defined as "a clear channel of running water." We could apply this same principle to our life. We want to have a consistent flow, free of stagnation. It's pure and running without hindrances. Joseph was one of my favorite saints because no matter the resistance that tried to come up against him, he stayed in the spirit. How many of us would allow our siblings to mistreat us the way his brothers treated him? But you see, Joseph had vision; he believed what the spirit of the Lord had prompted in his spirit…. Those that try to speak words contrary to the word of God will not prosper. They threw everything at him but the kitchen sink, but he was determined to stay in a spirit of Love. You must be persistent in your quest for destiny to receive the blessing. The enemy will try to annihilate you, but you are persuaded that we will assassinate the devil with our spiritual weapons. We see in the book of Genesis that Potiphar's wife tried to entice him to come to bed with her. But Joseph saw the enemy working through her. He denied her advances, and this completely disarmed Satan's strategy to take him out. In the end he was thrown into prison, but even in this place he was granted divine favor. Note: when opposition is at hand, Satan himself knows that your promotion is near. But here's where we have missed it. But I decree no more will we fail the test. What test? Remaining in the Spirit of Christ. Secondly, had Joseph taken Potiphar's wife up on her advances, he would not have walked in the favor that had been ordained for his life Romans 9–17.

Persecution will be a part of this promotion. God still is in control. Be Steadfast Genesis 39:11, 12, 13. We see the spirit of seduction operating in Potiphar's wife: she was scheming to set Joseph up through her own lustful desires. The Bible said that Joseph was a handsome man.... She had a husband that could have given her everything she wanted, but no—there was a seducing spirit in operation. Be on alert to this demon. Especially married couples. He had great discernment—he recognized the enemy's tactics to try and set him up. She seduced him, he rejected her...even though she had his cloak that was left behind to falsely accuse him with evidence. God said it doesn't matter what the enemy tries to use—people you work with, your loved ones.... Pass the test.... What's on the other side?......... PROMOTION. Joseph was falsely accused and was granted access to Manifested Power!

Companies, businesses are prospering because you are

there Genesis 39:20. Was what? With him.... That settles it....
If God be for you, who can dare be against you? Don't allow
power to leave you because of jealousy; sometimes we have to
let others be right to keep peace.... May I say this takes a lot
of prayer, fasting, and obedience.... It tries your character. The
Bible says, "blessed are the peacemakers for they shall inherit
the earth." Pray for the haters, naysayers, backbiters.... God
will see to it that you are blessed because of your love walk....
In Genesis 41:8, God granted Joseph power that no others had;
he was highly esteemed. Not only did Joseph have favor, he had
interpretations of dreams. No one in the provinces of this time
could interpret dreams. Remember, the anointing rested on
him because of his love walk for his adversaries.... This takes
character!!!! God had not left him—why? Joseph was always
on point. When the king called for him to give the interpretations, he did not have time to get ready. He was prepared to
give the summarization of his dreams. There will also be people
of high positions that will get promotion although they have
no revelation, no insight, no clue about kingdom things, and
God will give you insight of a project that only you knew. In
Genesis 40:8, 9: Let me prove it. The cupbearer **could not**
decipher dreams. People know when you have the gift. What
did he (Joseph) tell the cupbearer in Genesis 40:14? Remember
when he said "remember me"; Joseph told him that. Isn't it
amazing how people will use you for their good. Remember
me and mention to Pharaoh and get me out of prison; I have
done nothing wrong. He was in fact trying to take credit for
the interpretation of the dream. But God will still bless you in
the presence of your enemies. He will see to it that we get what
we should in our truthfulness. We have to begin to understand
"The Call": you are in a position to surrender all. Your life

is not your own anymore. This gospel is going to have to be preached with boldness, confidence, clarity, to be reached globally to win the end time of souls. I realize my life is no longer mine. I've given up the world's way of doing things and adopted God's economy. I announce to the Bailout I don't qualify because of the kingship anointing that I am walking in. We must purposely get bothered. God told me back in 2007 to get bothered; I did not fully understand the fullness of it but I do now. My life belongs to Him. God but my money is funny. "Get Bothered" meaning "Kingdom Business." My children are acting up. God says, "Get bothered." Lose the "But" and Loose your Manifested Power. It's available. Tap into it today. Stay focused. Be alert…. Be about His business; everything else will be added. He is a just God and he will never fail us. This is a Promise. Prayer: Father, we declare that we are blessed going in, blessed coming out. We are your workmanship in progress. We are walking victoriously in the things of our Father. He is a just God. Promotion is at hand. We receive all that our hands have labored for; because we are tithers we are blessed to be a blessing. The enemy will not destroy our crops, according to Malachi 3…. SATAN, you are rebuked. The Lord rebukes you. Back up: I have A Seed…. It is finished. We have authority over the princes of the air…. We receive all by faith in Jesus' name. Amen.

Empowered by the Power

"Not aborting God's Promises from Flowing into Manifestation"

I CAN REMEMBER a long time ago, I was thinking to myself I will try and be arrogant. I want to be what people used to call us: Stuck Up.... But you see, this was not God's plan of action for my life. The truth of it was it was a spirit of Pride operating. The Bible declares that Jesus resists the proud. He is not pleased when we allow this spirit to consume us. It separates us from the Love of Christ Ephesians 4:22. **"Therefore, the prisoner of the Lord, beseech you that ye walk worthy of the vocation wherewith ye are called, with lowliness and meekness, with longsuffering, forbearing one another in love."** We understand what Paul was talking about to the church of Ephesus. But if we read the word in Ephesians chapter 2, verse 4, Paul says, **"But God, who is** rich in mercy, for his great love wherewith he loved us. Even when we were dead in sins, hath quickened us together with Christ, (by grace ye are saved)." We see here our works alone will not save us. We must come boldly to the throne of grace to receive God's mercy. Do not allow the enemy to dictate his plan for your life. We have been adopted into the faith in his son Christ Jesus. We will have the promises to flow into our natural realm to be an example of God's promises in our life to minister souls in the end-time harvest. Be completely humble and Gentle. Proverbs 15:33: **"The fear of the Lord is the instruction of wisdom; and before honour is humility."** This pleases God when we are upright before him. Remember, if you miss the mark repent, and move on for the Kingdom of God. Romans 8:1 **"There is therefore now no condemnation to them which are in Christ Jesus, who walk not after the flesh, but after the Spirit."** Be patient bearing one another in Love. While we are waiting for our promises, we must learn to wait on God and not get in a hurry to rush the process. I remember times in my life when I would always want to get everything so fast. Each time I went ahead of God, it never turned out the way that I had expected. Listen to the leading of the Holy Spirit; he will never fail you. Many are busy talking to God about supplication and petitions, but do we really wait and listen to the things he desires to share with his children? Remove those hindrances and really press in and hear what God is saying to you. James 5:6: **"Be patient therefore, brethren unto the coming of the Lord."** Prayer and fasting will defuse the attacks of the adversary. This will also help us to tap into the mysteries of the kingdom that God will release into our spirits. You must develop a relationship with the Father to commune with him and him with you. This is true intimacy. It's a beautiful thing. Ask God to help you go deeper in him. Remember, he will never force himself on you. Surrender All. It's So Worth It. Let's take a journey together…. See you on the other side…of Glory….

DILIGENCE WITH A MISSION

DILIGENCE IS DEFINED as "hard, careful work; willingness or ability to work steadily and carefully plan." Being a diligent planner takes planning. You must first know what it is you are after. Secondly, have a plan of action to obtain the project you are assigning yourself to master. Be careful in this area not to share too much vital information in this area. Remember the **Blessing Blockers**; you do not need any hindrances in this Mission. Trust me, I can talk very well on this subject. I remember when we were on a mission in our home buying process. My husband and I agreed collectively we would not share this until the keys were in our hands. And you know what? It went much smoother. Had we gone ahead and told the world, I'm not so sure if the outcome would have been the same. For major purchases, this principle needs to be applied.... It works. Proverbs 12:24: **"The hand of the diligent shall bear rule, but the slothful shall be under tribute."** It is a blessing to be diligent rather than a lazy person. I believe it pleases our Father when we are blessing the Kingdom and being a blessing with our Gifts and Talents. Proverbs 13:4: **"The soul of the slug-gard desireth, and hath nothing. But the soul of the diligent shall be made fat."** *Persistence* is defined as "determination; a lasting continuous existence, to continue firmly in spite of opposition warning difficulty." I think this sums me up at this point in my life. Everything by the enemy had come to try and destroy me. Challenges writing this book, obstacles to set me back. This is the word for me.... Look at what it reads: "IN SPITE OF OPPOSITION"; that means it doesn't matter— you must push. I was told that I have a Push Ministry; I challenge saints of God to come up higher. Don't quit. Satan will never quit, but we are determined with everything in us that he will NOT win this battle.... Jesus has already overthrown the kingdom of darkness. In the Gospel of Luke the blind man, the beggar who sat by the side of the road, was persistent to get Jesus' attention. In verse 41 Jesus is saying, **"What wilt thou that I shall do unto thee? And he said, Lord that I may receive my sight. And Jesus said unto him, Receive thy sight. Thy faith hath saved thee."** His faith created the miracle that he needed to walk in his healing. This is the same anointing that we have for whatever miracle that we need.

Get Your House in Order: Spiritual and Natural Housecleaning....

Many of us have been so busy working, trying to provide a level of living, not realizing that if we are so busy with idleness, this can be an open door to our homes and our lives. Let us now Shut the door on the enemy. I believe before we can spiritually cast the devil out of our homes, we must first clean our homes. Yes, I mean we are going to clean up naturally. Go now to Wal-Mart, Dollar General, or wherever and buy some cleansing products and purify your homes. Uncleanliness is not an option. Clutter: remove it. How can you pray effectively if your home is a mess? If Jesus said that he is coming back in the flesh, how do you know that your home will not be his stop?... Something to consider exactly. Once you have tackled that, now you are ready for the Spiritual Cleaning. Remove the environment of Unclean Spirits before you begin this process; don't begin too fast. This requires some spiritual prepping before you go into this arena. Get your armor on for other demonic strongholds that could be setting up camp in your place of residency. Wickedness is in high places: bitterness, resentment, and strife Ephesians 4:31. Demons know who we are, so when we come, come with the thunder which is the sword of the spirit. Take authority over the forces of darkness and declare to that devil the very elect words that Jesus told him after tempting him after the forty-day fast. It is written. "Enough said." There must be consecration. What does it mean to consecrate? It means to be set apart and remain in the presence of God. Ask the Holy Spirit to guide you into all truths. Exodus 13:1: The Lord told Moses to go into the land flowing with milk and honey. There has to be sacrificing to go in and possess. Verse 6 decrees that the Canaanites, the Hittites, the Amorites—all the "ITES"—had to fast for seven days on unleavened bread. This is bread that has no yeast…. Can I be honest? I asked my husband about this bread since he is anointed in this area. This bread has bacteria? What is that exactly? It means that the bread was deemed unclean. One must also keep the Sabbath Holy. I've noticed when I truly Honor the Sabbath, my week at a glance tends to go more smoothly. Not saying there aren't any challenges, just fewer. Exodus 31:13 Unforgiveness: Please, saints of God, we have to get this right. Repent of any offenses? Who does she think she is? Don't allow Satan's grip to get your destiny aborted through this sin. Search your heart and forgive, release, so God can replenish and restore Psalms 103:3; Matthew 6:12; Luke 23:34. Start at verse 28. Spiritual Protocol: Who are you being accountable to? Yes, God is the head, but for those of us that are married, the husbands are the head. This doesn't mean that we are less, but this is the order of God. We have been commanded by our Lord and Savior to submit; on the other hand, men have to step into their rightful positions as the heads of house and lead, lead, lead. Which leads me to my next point: Submission Genesis 21; Ephesians 5:22. Just as Christ gave himself to the church, so shall the men of God love their wives as Christ has graciously loved us. Anoint thy dwelling place, cover your homes, cars, businesses, anywhere your soles tread, and have the confidence and faith that at the commanded spoken word of God, things have to change. Anoint your furnishings, dwelling, etc. Proverbs 18:21; Genesis 17:1. We must commune with God daily in prayer—not only petitioning or supplications, but we must be patient and allow the Holy Spirit to whisper points of power into our spirit. Remember, stay still; God will speak if we only listen. This requires patience. Spiritual download: God gave me this word back in 2007; allow points that are inspired from God to have free liberty to be planted inside of your spirit. These are his visions and dreams so you may excel in everything you touch. And your plans shall be established. If God has given you that assignment, he will certainly equip you to reach the goals that are set before you.

UNCHARTED TERRITORY

JUST RECENTLY I visited a Land that in my opinion is untapped territory. It is in need of a revival. And Suddenly there was a loud roar in the upper room—the people were from all facets of Life. At random they were all in one accord. (See Acts.) It is amazing how the Holy Spirit speaks to us. Maybe he has given you an assignment as well. You cannot begin to understand God's process for bringing it to pass. The Lord revealed to me that I will live in Albuquerque, New Mexico, for a season. Just a few weeks ago, my foot landed upon the grounds of this land. Never been there before; don't know anyone there. Just like God told Joshua and Caleb that they would go in and possess the Land. You can surely have it. Don't do the "what ifs." What ifs might not even happen; then what? You could have possibly missed out on a wealth of territory by not obeying the voice of the Lord. Who am I talking to? Go into the land and take back everything that the enemy has stolen. If he said it, he shall equip you with the tools to perform his work for his glory. I am a living Testimony…. Soar…and Go…. I obeyed the voice of the Lord and I booked the plane ticket. I heard the audible voice say "buy ticket today." I obeyed and within two days I was airborne. That in itself was God; you don't purchase a ticket on that short notice and not spend close to a thousand dollars. The trip was a fraction of that amount. The amazing part is not the trip, but how easily it happened. Saints of God, he has anointed each and every one of you for greatness, and he wants to watch us climb these mountains. How much God wants to give good gifts to those who obey him. The key is to listen and move when the cloud is moving. Be in the timing of God. This is where the promises are. I was told that the land was full of Witchcraft. No problem—God will perform his miracles through signs and wonders. Those people (witches) will fall to their knees and cry out to the Lord and come with a heart of repentance. You must also pray for sharp discernment to know when you are among wolves. We must begin to pray that the spirit of the Lord is everywhere, and I believe Salvation will come to them as well. Revival, Revival, Revival…. Defilement will not last; there is no good thing that will become of living on the wrong path. Destruction will tear you down. God will not force himself upon anyone; he will give each and every one of us our free will. Choose Christ. It has been such an amazing Journey; I am excited about the Bride of Christ going higher for the Glory of God.

People are watching—I mean unbelievers—to see how we handle adversity. Will we fold under pressure? Will we lose self-control? Or will we say, "Okay, God, this is the hand that I have been dealt; I know you have all power in your hand and you can turn the storms into sunshine"? We have to believe that he is in complete control. Trust him at all times and lean not unto thine own understanding. Even when things are not looking in thy favor, know that God's got our back and his will never fails…. Heaven and Earth will pass away, but the word of the Lord will stand any test or adversity. There are times when people will not understand what you are about. I know this now in my life. All hell has broken loose in my life; it's as though "God, are you with me?"—but you see, my friends, my faithfulness is not predicated on how many tangible things I can have. You see, God wants to know. Do you really Love him? Will you serve him in the good and bad? It doesn't really require great faith: if things are well, you have a little money in the bank. The true test is will you go ALL the way with God. I believe that is what he wants: our true love for him. God is a merciful God; he has never left us. The truth is some of us have left him. But Jehovah Jireh will provide everything that we need and more. Be found being about your Father's business.

Blinders Removed...

As you begin to go into this place, you must begin to look not as the world looks at things. I make it a point daily to **NOT** become consumed with the Doom and Gloom bailout dilemma on television. Saints of God, be guarded with what becomes captive of your eyes. I believe this can easily cause us to get our eyes off our promise with too much negativity. Look to the Hills.... God's plan will never be bailout. We will be blessed and highly favored because of our obedience to our tithes and seed sowing; with these principles activated, we will succeed and have guaranteed return on our investments. When I speak of the blinders being removed, as we walk with the Lord we don't see as we once did—we are new creatures. The scales must begin to fall off so we can see clearly through lenses of faith. Processing this to happen will require pure dedication of the renewing of your mind. Feed your faith with the Word. Do not let up until change is possessed. We have the faith to believe that everything that we petition The Father plans shall come to pass according to his will. So I encourage you to pray the word with boldness and power over your situation, and heaven will get in on the plan for your future success. Pray until you lay hold of it; confess until the manifestation is AT HAND.... Once you receive, don't let go; continue to stretch yourself for your next level. Never give place to stagnation. Dear God, I realize that I may have once had blinders on my eyes that I could not see because of possible unbelief, fear, anxiety, worry, or other obstacles. But today I announce to myself that I am free, free, free; no longer am I bound by the cares of this world. I surrender all to your feet, Jesus. I renounce every evil attack that has been assigned to try and abort my destiny. I cancel you at the root and command you by the blood covenant of Christ to Loosen your hold over God's property now, In Jesus' Name. It Is Done!!! Now get your Praise ON.... WE WIN.

The Dream of Unseen
Resources...

FOR THOSE OF you who don't know how to hold fast to your confession without wavering, you must really be on your level to discern and hear quickly. By this it simply means, when you pray no matter what happens HOLD ON! The book of Deuteronomy, chapter 28:1, states, **"And it shall come to pass, if thou shalt hearken diligently unto the voice of the Lord thy God, to observe and to do all his commandments which I command thee this day, that the Lord thy God will set thee on high above all nations of the earth. 2. And all these blessings shall come on thee, and overtake thee, if thou shall hearken unto the voice of the Lord thy God."** This is a promise; how can you hearken? What does it mean to hearken? *Webster's* defines the word *hearken* as to listen or to pay attention to. Wow, this is good. Do you see the connection? We have to pay attention to what the spirit of the Lord is revealing to his children. If God has given you a dream or vision and you say, "Bridgett, there is no way I will be able to afford this vision," I would say to you that it's a good indication that this can be God. Because the truth is this is exactly how he gets the Glory. If he told you to do a specific assignment, it is his obligation to work it out to get the resources channeled to you. This is why it so imperative that we don't try to self-promote ourselves; allow the Holy Spirit to do the leading at all times. One day I was driving after being off for some months when the spirit of the Lord revealed to me to quit my job. Now saints of God, I must admit I debated with God. I was making decent money, and things were beginning to really look up for me and my family. In obedience I sided of course with the voice of God, and left my assignment of close to three years. God revealed that I was about two months outside of disobedience, but the truth was I believe I battled with fear, or how I was going to provide for the things that had to be paid—or so I thought. I stepped out on faith. One month later, my husband came home and told me that he had just gotten laid off. My initial reaction was, okay, God, did I miss you or was this now going to be our marital faith test? Long story short: this was the best sabbatical that I could have asked for. We were able to eat lunch daily. I believe something was rekindled in us. There were years where I could safely say we were just passing because of our careers. But God has a way of bringing us to complete humility and divine trust in him. The truth is he wants us to depend solely on his love and grace. How can we do this if we always want to be in control? Today I say surrender, Let Go, and Let the master lead you beside the still waters. There is peace in this level.... I had developed headaches daily before leaving my last assignment, and

I asked God why and he revealed to me because what I called you to do, I have appointed you to do. You were in error because that assignment had lifted. His anointing was no longer on me for that location. So therefore I was consequently in my flesh. I reaped the things of the flesh such as headaches, fatigue, etc. The cloud had lifted according to Exodus 40:34: **"Then a cloud covered the tent of the congregation and the glory of the Lord filled the tabernacle. And Moses was not able to enter the tent of the congregation because the cloud abode thereon, and the glory of the Lord filled the tabernacle. And when the cloud was taken up over the tabernacle the children of Israel went onward in all their journeys."** You must be able to discern when to hold and when to let go…. This comes through relationship and fasting. If the brook has dried up, this might be a factor that God has moved from that place. I believe that a once blessed place can become a stagnant place. Do not try to make something happen when God is telling you to move onward. Journey ahead…. Trust him and he will show you the way…. If you still cannot discern, this will be a good time to go into a fast for clear direction.

THE SPIRITUAL
BAILOUT PLAN...

BLESSINGS WILL BE on those who walk uprightly before the Lord. I tell the precious saints that I minister too that God is not on a Bailout Plan. We are the King's children, and because we have obeyed the instructions of this word we shall reap a harvest; how could it be that I have recently opened up a new Hair Salon No. 5? In the natural this should **NOT** be happening. But I've decided to purposely put pressure on this word. I will be successful. I will have what I declare. My children will be mighty in the Land. According to Psalm 112, speak the word only until you lay hold of it. I don't agree with what this economy is telling me. Not so... Not so. I choose to PURPOSELY lay hold of this word. I will not listen to the naysayer of this world system. Don't allow poison to enter your mindset via the television, radio, etc. I realize we must be informed on worldviews, but please don't allow this to pollute your spirit man. I suggest after watching the news to pray in the Holy Ghost to edify your spirit man. Note: we want our spiritual man to be more advanced than our flesh man.... We have a promise according to Deuteronomy 7–14: **"Thou shalt be blessed above all people: there shall not be male or female barren among you, or among your cattle."** We will never go without if we hearken unto the voice of the Lord; obey and try not to lean unto thy own understanding. Believe all things are possible. Jesus has already paid the death penalty for our sins. Just obey.... Our lives will be so much more fulfilling when we live by the foundation of the biblical principles. Do not try to reinvent the wheel, so to speak. This manual will yield huge profits...seedtime and harvest. Sow your seed; put a specific assignment for it and watch God Bless you like never before. Remember to pay your tithes first. You can't be a sower and not be a tither; this is **NOT** God's law. Tithe is always first. This keeps the curse off of you. The seed over the tithe is for the Harvest. I need both; what about you? We will be diligent with our giving. In your giving, expect things to change. We will be blessed because of the obedience of the tithe. Malachi 3 is the covenant blessing scripture; don't take away or add to it.

Journaling Ahead
for the Prize...

How many of us have had a thought that has come to mind, and in an instant it was gone? We've tried to recover it in our minds to no avail; it seems so far. Journaling is getting the thoughts on paper. Writing the things that God is giving you is so important. We need to have a blueprint of the future. In Habakkuk 2:2 it simply says to write the vision and make it plain on tablets. This is so vital so as not to lose recall. I always say I need my brain so I don't try to remember things; that's why we have paper.... Use them. This brings the vision in clearer and into perspective because of the journaling. Also, the Holy Spirit will give you spiritual insight on strategies for your life. I have received so much insight from writing down my thoughts. Releasing your emotions on paper is so lifting to your spirits. Many visions from entrepreneurs have become a reality through a napkin or sheets of scrap paper. I remember one day I was sitting at my salon dryer chair and the Lord gave me my dream that would become a reality. I began to draw and the Holy Spirit guided my hand. After the completion of it, I thought to myself, God, only you could do this because one, I don't profess to be a great drawer. See yourself in this next place. Keep a piece of tablet on the side of the bed for those that dream in the night. If you don't have the gift of interpreting the dreams, I invite you to ask God to bless you with this wonderful gift. Genesis 40 Go ahead and pen away—write, write, write. The Bible says the people perish without the vision. He wants you to have it. Our Father desires to give his children great gifts. Go for it; if it is a Million-dollar dream like I have, there is nothing too hard for God…. Partner with God and Soon Your Dreams will become a reality.

I'm Still Standing...
and So Are You

Many times the enemy will try to completely shoot his best shot at you. Sometimes there have been times when I think okay, God, you allowed me to come through that storm.... Some storms seem as though the weather will never cease and you look up and there is the sun. God is so gracious in how he preps us for the opposition. I think about my son Cedric; he is a warrior. His name actually means "Chief" and he is indeed that fighter. He has endured so much at such a young age. As parent's you want to reach out and take the blows and abuse that the enemy tries to deal your children. But you see, just as God gave us his only son Jesus, we need to know that God will allow us to go through trials to make us stronger. Cedric has had awesome jobs and not-so-good jobs, yet in the middle of the fire he seems to take it blow after blow. In the natural my spirit is crying out for him, but you see he is my natural son, and God loves him dearly. God is perfecting him, allowing him to grow up and be the Man of God he was destined to be. One day I received a call and he was in a dilemma, and I, wanting to be Supermom, decided that I would run across town to rescue him, and God spoke to my heart: are you going to save him or do you want me to? I thought to myself, WOW. I quickly repented, turned my vehicle around, and drove back home. The truth is if I would have put my hand in it, God would have taken his hands off of it. God told me, "I am Lord over Cedric." Since then I do not intervene, I pray for him, and I allow the correction to come from the throne room because he is a man now. I will not cripple him in his walk. Cedric was created in his image. No matter what I think he should be, Jesus sees him as blessed and he's highly favored of the Lord. He's a strong man, but I still see him as my baby. There was a time when he was a young boy and he was diagnosed with ADD (Attention Deficit Disorder), and I spent thousands of dollars trying to figure out what was wrong—through the guilt and hurt of blaming myself, thinking why was this happening to me as a parent? I had consumed myself with working all of the time. I felt that I should have been there for him. But you see, at that time I was a single parent trying to provide for my son. What he wanted from me was not the latest video game or gadget; he needed me. Over time of the pain, I had to forgive myself and realize I did the best that I could under those present circumstances. The medications would zombie him to the point of him losing his appetite. I was depressed and in need of a savior. I needed God to step in and take control. It was during this time that I was filled with the Holy Spirit. I was saved, but I knew if I was to fight this demonic stronghold, I needed that power of anointing, that was freely available for me to tap into. Nothing but the blood of Jesus could wash away all my guilt. I will never forget one night when I was watching TBN and I asked the Lord to reveal himself to me if he was this person. Jesus promised that after he was ascended back to heaven, he would send us a comforter. My life began to transform into this beautiful shape. It was years of purging, praying, and fasting. I had so much junk that was imbedded in me. But saints of God, he was there for me every step of the way. And for anyone who thinks that he will not help you out of any temptation, HE CAN and HE WILL…I am living proof. Prayer: Father, help me to heal from anything that has tried to hinder my walk in you. Forgive me for not allowing you to be Lord over my life, but instead I've chosen in error to do things my way. The truth is it will never work.… Meet me at this location. God, here I am Saved by Grace; thank you, Father, for being my Redeemer and Healer In Jesus' Name, Amen. No matter the obstacle or the trial, this one thing I know is that I will dwell in the House of the Lord forever. Amen. Search your hearts and release the sin that will separate you from your relationships with God. He loves you and will meet you at whatever level you are on. Don't allow the enemy to play tricks with your mind. You blew it this time; he will never forgive you for that. NO, that's the lie of Satan. There is no such thing as a big sin. Sin is Sin—it separates us from God. That is why we should repent daily when we miss it. We are more than conquerors. We are well equipped to handle any adversity that comes at us.… Dig your heels in and shout with a great sound of Zion. You will come out of this battle victoriously. What an awesome God we serve. It's not over until God says it's over.

ENLARGE MY TERRITORY

I DECLARED SOME time ago that I wanted to have all that God had for me. No matter what the circumstances. I decided I am SOLD OUT for Christ. Friends of God, we must develop this warrior mentality to get to this place. Like Jabez said in Chronicles, **"OH, that You would bless me indeed, and enlarge my territory, that Your hand would be with me and that You would be with me, and that You would keep me from evil."** Let's examine the first sentence. Jabez comes boldly to the throne and makes a command to God: "That you would bless me indeed." I'm sure he had daily issue problems, challenges that were up against him. He did not say, "Oh Lord, if it's your will Bless me." NO, he makes a declaration to God. I feel we must know by faith when we come to God, who is INDEED our Father, that we believe with our mouths to pray in faith the prayer of faith petitions, knowing if we pray according to the word that he hears us. Let's dissect the Second verse:

"ENLARGE MY TERRITORY".... He wants the Kingdom; this is in fact the calling. What has God been instructing you to do? Have you asked God about your calling? If you don't know, then ask The Holy Spirit to reveal to you what your assignment in the world would be. Prayer: Lord, I come boldly to the throne in faith. Father, I want to be all that you have created me to be. Help me to discern my calling in you. I commit myself completely to the Kingdom of God, and I want to be obedient and step into my anointing that you have for me to be a blessing for your Glory in Jesus' name Yea thou I walk through the valley of the shadow of death, I will fear No evil for thou art with me...Amen. Thirdly, in this passage of scripture it reveals that your hand will be with me; it is clear that what he anoints, he appoints—his hand will be with you on this journey. Be obedient to hear his voice and move when he speaks. Do not try to operate fleshly emotions to render kingdom answers. That's like Night and Day—they are completely opposite. Lastly, this scripture states that he will keep us from evil; this is his promise of divine intervention to the forces of hell. God will protect us in our assignments. So don't worry about the enemy—he is a defeated foe, and No weapon that is formed against you shall prosper. Even when it does not look like things are moving, you have to believe by faith that the awesome hand of God is with you to the end. I believe the greatest miracles are worked over or created our darkest hours of life. Character is always being developed in this time. God will anoint you to do the work that he has called you to do. Once you pass what I call the faith test, he will elevate you to your next level. Promotion in the spirit realm is granted when we are promoted in the obstacles that try to offset us. Know that we have to stay strong in the Lord and be fully persuaded that we will stand firm on the word. Conquering the giants in this level will be your advancement to go higher in God. So never fret in your circumstances, Keep a positive attitude, and you will go from Glory to Glory....

UNFUNDED DREAMS...
GOD WILL FUND HIS PLAN

ONE DAY BACK in October, I had been working at this salon in Atascocita. I had leased a space there for about two and a half years. The Lord had told me to go there because I had work to do there. I was working on another side of Houston. However, out of obedience and not having any clients and having to pay double the amount of my rent, I went there; God said to me it's not about you, but I am using you as an instrument. But you see, God was concerned about me. As I began to minister to the ladies there, my business began to grow; you see I was storing up seeds of faith, and the harvest was phenomenal. My business doubled the first year there. Each month my business would peak more and more. God was teaching me the importance of Patience. Allowing the Holy Spirit to lead and guide me into all truths. I yielded to his voice and obediently went. In the beginning, of me moving to the new location, there were days and days I would sit there and not have any clients. But God was teaching me patience, and persistence. The Holy Spirit would instruct me to pray on other people's behalf. I'm thinking to myself, God, how can you tell me to pray and I can barely pay the rent in this salon? The Lord received the Glory of affirmation, and I was tremendously blessed in the assignment. We live in this microwavable society. If it's fast, easy, quick, that is what we want. But I believe that the blessing is in the obedience. God had the plan for my life in that season.... I had an assignment to fulfill, and I wanted to please God. I had developed a mentality of excellence in the Kingdom. I wanted with everything in me to please The Father. I met some amazing women and men in that location. I witnessed amazing miracles, healings, and deliverances in this unusual setting for the gospel. I know now we are not bound by the four walls of a Sanctuary. It is everywhere our feet treads. We have taken this message of the Gospel into the marketplace. I believe the greatest revivals are going to happen in unusual places. Watch and See; we will see the signs and wonders. Nevertheless, there came a time when the brook had dried up. My business was continuing to flourish, but the well at that place was not flowing for me. There was spiritual darkness that had overcome the environment. I had indeed come to the end of that journey in the call. I began to experience migraine headaches. God revealed to me, "I am no longer anointing you to handle the warfare in this place." I was in complete error, and what was normally working for me no longer rendered results. I sought the Lord and fasted and he told me to move.... We had a storm that hit the Gulf Coast—Hurricane Ike—and the Lord had told me to leave that place. I did not want to obey because the truth is I needed to make some Christmas money, so I thought. But you see I still was operating in my flesh, because I believe my blessing was in the salon chair. Jesus is saying to someone, "Step out, I will take your hand and guide you." The spirit of the Lord spoke to me and told me you can stay here and try to make this little money behind this chair or you can leave and completely trust me in this next journey. I still tarried with what God was telling me; I thought God, I have to make a living—how can I do this?... But I thought, God, you have never left me; I trust you in this too. My husband completely did not understand. In fact he never told me, but he thought that I had lost my natural mind. I said, "Ernest, I feel a strong call to leave my job." He was like, "OK Bridgett, are you sure?" I replied, "Yes, I really feel this in my spirit." I'm stepping; I could no longer deal with the unstableness in my thinking at that time.... So I left. May I say this was the best time in our marriage.... The children were so happy; they would say, "My mom is not working anymore...Yeahh...." They were so ecstatic. I thought okay, I can't spend money frivolously; we will be on a budget. That was a joke—BUDGET, what is that? I was so happy.... How could someone not having a job have this much joy? I don't know. I believe it was the joy of the Lord. I also believe I was in burnout of my life.Wife, Mother, Minister, Hair Stylist,—you know all the labels every woman in America is wearing. God was completely faithful to us as he is always. We trusted in our Lord and Savior and he met us at our every need. What is God telling you to step into? Can I say that he will confirm every word that he has spoken to you? If he has given you the green light on any assignment, trust him—he will provide every single aspect of the promise. He is no respecter of persons. If he could do this thing for me and my family, I know he will meet you with every detail of what he has anointed you to do for his glory. Prayer: Father, I ask you to quicken our spirit of this newfound revelation concerning our dreams and visions for our life. Remove any hindrance, doubt, and fear to go higher in the things of God. I accept your perfect will of God in my life. Take control of this driver seat and I will yield to you, Father; I will not fear what man can do to me. Because you said that the greater one is working on the inside of me. Reveal yourself, Master to me like never before. I receive this newfound revelation In Jesus' Name, Amen.

THE HOLDING PATTERN

MANY TIMES IN life we go into what I call a holding pattern. It appears as though things are going in full circle as though we are not going to ever land. We need to readjust our mindsets and trust that God is in the driver's seat and he will never fail us. You say, "But Prophetess B, my life seems as if it is out of control." If this is you that I am talking to, perhaps you need a readjustment of how you are viewing the promises of God. If he said it, we shall have all that he has intended for us to have in our lives, blessed abundantly. In the book of Matthew, the word declares that the violent take it by force. We see that this means this is no place for Complacency.... You must be radical in your stand. The enemy is not going to give you anything... without a fight. Know that with prayer and supplications you can win. I used to hear the old saints say, "BABY, God won't put any more on you than you can bear." I beg to differ. There have been times in my life where I wanted to scream. Like

God, have you put this load on me? But the truth is he wants me and you to exercise faith muscles and build them so we can endure so when the next storm comes, we can overcome. It's going from Faith to Faith, Glory to Glory. This way he gets the glory for our victories. I always say Man will not take God's place. We have to lean and depend on him, and the truth is that is how I live now. I can remember losing my hair, skin breaking out because of Unbelief. I remember one day when I said, wait a minute. No longer will I tarry with these thoughts or emotions. I need to enter into the rest of God. I was handling my problems in the carnal (sin) nature and Jesus is saying cast this over to him…for he will be able to carry this load far better than we can. Take no thought of what we should eat. I remember recently I was standing in the salon with this awesome view of the city. I noticed a bird on the ground. As I stood there I thought, it's 100 degrees outside, and I realized what Matthew 6 really meant. This bird did not worry about I'm thirsty, it sure is hot out here. I'm sure that morning when he woke up, he probably ate worms, etc. I thought we need to be like the birds and COMPLETELY trust him for our daily provisions. Let us not be like the children in Egypt murmuring and complaining. Enter into the rest of God.… Prayer: Lord Jesus, help us to take our hands off of the things that we place ahead of you. Help us to allow you to be our pilot and guide us into all truths of your word. Father, we renounce fear, worry, negative mindsets, wrong thinking. We believe for every manifested promise and provision that you have for us. Forgive us for not allowing you to guide us because of our own agendas. We thank you in advance for being our ever-present help in times of trouble. Amen.

"Let It Reign"

THIS IS NOT some cliché that people sometimes use—this is God's word. The word declares that if we suffer with him, we will reign with him. What exactly does that mean? You see, going through the suffering will produce patience. How do you think Christ felt on the cross when he died on the Cross? I feel that he suffered at that time, the bed of thorns being placed on his head. Christ died for our sins. How God selflessly gave up his only begotten son. I pondered on that the other day when I was engaged in a conversation with someone and they indicated, "Would you give up your children?" Immediately my mind begins to think on Abraham when he was about to slay Isaac on the altar. I began to really examine my own heart. I thought God, do I really mean that I would do anything for you, because the truth is would you give up your very own (children) for obedience to him? If we are honest with ourselves, I believe the answer would be NO. But I believe also the parallel of the story in Genesis 22:11: "And the angel of the Lord called unto him out of heaven; and said, Abraham, Abraham: and he said, Here am I. (verse 12) And he said '**Lay not thine hand upon the lad, neither do thou anything unto him: for now I know that thou fearest God, seeing thou hast not withheld thy son, thine ONLY son from me.**" I believe that is the very obedience Jesus wants from us—to walk completely in the fullness of the promises, even if our own human understanding cannot comprehend the very nature of God. This requires complete trust in him. I thank God every day for sending his son Jesus to die for my sins. If you have children, which most people do, just imagine allowing someone to say to you, "Can I have your child to execute?" You would respond like, "You have to be serious?… You are crazy…." The devil is a liar…. He also had to be in an intimacy and complete oneness with God to know that the enemy was not deceiving him, despite these instructions. This also tells me that Isaac had a relationship with his master to understand the vital wisdom that God was telling him to do on that mountain. I also wonder if that's why Isaac went along with his lad and left the others behind. I can just hear them with Spiritual awareness saying something like, "Isaac, what are you doing? Are you out of your mind putting your son on the altar about to kill him?" We need to make sure we are listening to him for all of our instructions. Sometimes people don't understand the vision that he gives—I believe because it's not for them, it's for the person that he has promised it to. I've learned not to try to convince others on what the Holy Spirit has shared with you. Just do it…. Distractions can slow down the timing of God. I've learned that the less people know, the better. I always say, "They find out when they find out." God so graciously gave his only begotten son to be a blessing to us...so we can have Salvation; what an awesome God we serve. Eternal life was granted because of this selfless act. You have to be willing to pay a price for something worth having. Truth is, no one wants to suffer; I feel that this is where many believers have missed the mark. The word declares, "Many are the afflictions of the righteous but the Lord delivers us out of them all." Pastors often time will tell parishioners that oh, you will have prosperity, and that is true—God wants us to have the good fruits—but you will encounter trials and tribulations. I think this factor can be misleading because the truth is we will all encounter storms we will go through for the gospel, but be of good cheer: Jesus has overcome the world. I have complete assurance we will win if we don't give up. Keep yourself engulfed in the word and he will keep you. Surround yourself with the right people of faith who will help you in your battle fight. Negative friends will rob you and drain you of your energy. I read a sign recently that said, "Be a fountain, not a drain." I thought, wow that is good. I want to be a river that is flowing constantly with pure water. Not a drain that is clogged up with junk and not producing. I always say take the word into battle with you. Stay armored up. Confess in this arena until the promise is at hand. Don't be moved by your circumstances; this is a Faith Walk. Remember: Faith is NOT SEEING, but believing in your heart that God will do what he said he will do. By faith, Peter believed in the book of Mark that he would walk on Water, and as long as he stayed focused on the Prize Jesus was there.... By faith the Hebrew boys were thrown into the fiery furnace, and after the furnace was seven times hotter the Bible declared that they came out without any spots or blemishes. **By faith** the Red Sea opened up as the children of Israel crossed over into the promise. **By faith** God promised

Abraham and Sarah they would produce offspring in old age. **By faith** the Walls of Jericho came down. **By faith** Jeremiah prophesied as a little child. **By faith** Ezekiel said, "can dead bones live?" **By faith** Mary conceived Jesus, when the naysayers believed her NOT after the Holy Spirit impregnated her. What is your **"By Faith"** moment? Pray and God will reveal to you what your **BY FAITH** moment is.... We are walking in authority and boldness to take back everything the enemy has stolen from us, as well as our forefathers. You have to move into unfamiliar territory; that is how Faith is activated. We just have to go and possess, and God will show us the plan. When you move, GOD moves not the other way around. I have said it on countless times: I'm waiting on God. NO God is waiting on me. Move out of your comfort zone; allow the Holy Spirit to take you into greater heights that you know NOT of. If God has told you to do something that is in the natural impossible, I am willing to bet that it is possibly of God. Why do we need him if we can do it on our own? This is how he gets the Glory; he wants us to depend totally on him. I do not understand why God would tell me to move to Albuquerque, where I absolutely do not know anyone. Truth is, my flesh wants to stay here in Houston where I know all of the highways and byways. But this dream has been on the inside of me for some years now, but you see God will grant you a vision and he will give you the strategic plan of action...execution to bring it to pass. TRUST, HONOR, and OBEY in God's timing, not OURS.... He will hold fast to every assignment that he has called you to do. You must position yourself to stay in the face of God no matter what comes at you. If he has endorsed you, he will approve you too. Go into the Land to Possess for his GLORY.

POSITIONING FOR THE WIN

POSITIONING FOR THE win...finding what work will position you for the win. Athletes have to go to practice daily in order to enhance their fullest potential. When you are in position, there is a level of confidence that is in place. There is a level of expectancy when a football team has practiced for that big game. Do you think a team that never practices will ever win? The answer is probably not so. However, for those who have practiced, trained, and looked at past mistakes on a tape, these will certainly place that team in a better position for the win than an opposing opponent who never practices. This is true in the Spiritual Realm as well. You must practice on the field. How so? Glad you asked. Your field of prayer... Position yourself on your knees in the shower, in the car, in the kitchen, or wherever you meet the Lord; this is your weapon for battle. Exercise those spiritual muscles and allow the Holy Spirit to Stretch you. Stay in the Spirit.... Having an attitude of faith will help you to increase your Spiritual Discernment that trouble is brewing or trouble has Landed…. Let us not wait until trouble comes before we begin to exercise our Spiritual Muscles; we need them in action every day. Winning requires strategizing…. You must study your opponent—you have to study your opponent. We see that there is nothing new under the sun. If this is true, why are we constantly going around the same mountain and allowing the same trials and obstacles to defeat us? The enemy has no new tricks; it's the same routine. I've noticed in my own life if I am frustrated and easily irritated, my life seems to go into a spiral domino effect. But if I Purposely think NO, I am not going to go there, I will think on only those things that are pleasing to God. Stay in the positive mind zone. I can dismantle the enemy's schemes, and most of the time the problem will resolve itself or it may not be as it appears. Satan gets us off track through illusions… "Wrong stinking thinking." Renew your Mind Daily; Put on the Whole armor of God so we can stand against the wiles of the Devil. Do Not allow bitterness and anger to set in no matter what the circumstances are. I believe illnesses such as high blood pressure, cancers, and other ailments are from just NOT releasing people who have offended us rather than just allowing the Holy Spirit to soothe our hearts and enter into the forgiveness of God and release everyone who has violated us in one way or another. Truth is, why carry it? That person is possibly asleep or on vacation—someone not worrying about you. Today let's release whoever it is and take your power back…. Don't be controlled by negative emotions anymore. Invite the Holy Spirit to come in and soothe your soul. Do not allow our minds to take over our thought life…. Prayer: Father, help me to offer up forgiveness to those people that have offended me, and help me to stay free of any offence or hurt from others. I ask forgiveness as well if I have hurt or harmed anyone that maybe I know or do not know. Father, I receive your love that will cover a multitude of sins.... Thank you for this freedom in you in Jesus' name, Amen.... I see myself as God sees me more than a conqueror.... Positioning for the win takes walking in Love when others speak things to us that are not pleasing to our minds.... Think on what is of a good report...I choose to purposely meditate on God's spoken word of God.... Psalms 59:1: **"Deliver me from mine enemies O my God: defend me from them that rise up against me. Deliver me from the workers of iniquity, and save me from bloody men. For lo they lie in wait for soul: the mighty are gathered against me; not from my transgression, nor for my sin, O God. (verse 9) ... because of his strength will I wait upon thee: for God is my defence."**

NOT THY WILL BUT THOU WILL BE DONE...

ENTERING INTO THE rest of God has to become a great part of your daily life. Projects, Family, Careers, People, or any other things that will cause our primary focus to be taken, have to be placed into perspective. Begin to meditate on what is really important in life. I think if we begin to simplify our lives, we will see that what we believe is so important really isn't. You will begin to see you don't have to have that new pair of shoes when the truth is, you might have 50 pairs in your closet. God is speaking today to begin to purge away from the things that will try to steal the very essence of who you really are. I always say, stay grounded in the faith, knowing that if we keep our eyes on the prize we will win. The race is not given to the swift, but is given unto the one who endures to the end. I prophesy that every person reading this book will complete every assignment that Jesus has instructed him to begin…. Not only will you begin it, you will complete every task at hand that is in his plan for your life. Begin to ask God, what is your will for my life? I believe that many believers are out of God's will and his anointing are not on the assignment at hand for their life. How do you know that God's breath is not on something? Are you at complete peace there? Are you frustrated a lot when hell is breaking loose?… Do you experience migraine head-aches?… Do you have anxiety or stress? These are signs that you need to seek God on if you are in his Divine Will for your life. It could be that the season for that assignment has lifted. Therefore, you are reaping the fruits of the flesh. On the other hand, you could be in error because God has called you to do work and you are rebelling. Or maybe afraid to step out of your comfort zone. **"Rest in the Lord, and Wait patiently for him: fret not thyself because of him who prospereth in his way, because of the man who bringeth wicked devices to pass."** Keep your eyes on Jesus. Obey what the spirit of the Lord is speaking. If he allows the door to close, keep it closed; he knows what's best for us. Trust God and he will show you the pathway. Remain confident that we cannot see what's on the other side of obedience. Release the angels to go before you, and begin to prepare the way for the prize…. Do not fret….do not quit…. Keep yourself around faith-building people. When you truly begin to yield unto the Spirit of the Lord, then God is obligated to get involved in our future plans, because we have asked him to come in and show us the way. Remember if you give in to the flesh, you will reap to the flesh. This is a Spiritual Awakening…. Elijah told the widow woman to prepare him a meal in the natural. I'm sure she was thinking to herself God, let me prepare this final meal so my son and I can die. But she allowed faith to rise up on the inside of herself and see that her blessing was in HIS mouth. She obeyed the Prophet and she was restored.... What are you believing for today? Begin to surrender yourself completely unto God. He will order your steps. I often tell others, "Don't be legalistic about life." Have you ever been around people who know IT ALL? Truth is, I believe we all need to have a teachable spirit. We all want to look at the magnifying glass of our souls and enter into the realism of who we really are, and to know our truths. Truths will allow us to make changes to things that are not pleasing to the Lord.... Finally, I will conclude that being in a transparent state, recognizing truth and making necessary changes within oneself can we truly enter into Divine Power with Manifested Power. God Bless and enjoy this journey called THERE.

CPSIA information can be obtained
at www.ICGtesting.com
Printed in the USA
LVOW08s1844180617
538521LV00001B/126/P